The Ghosts of Reginald Hine

An Uncommon Attorney

THE GHOSTS OF
REGINALD HINE

An Uncommon Attorney

R<small>ICHARD</small> W<small>HITMORE</small>

MATTINGLEY PRESS

Published by the Mattingley Press
Hitchin, Hertfordshire SG4 7NH
Richard Whitmore © 2007
Epilogue Andrew McEwen © 2007

ISBN 978 0 9554662 0 5

Designed and typeset in Adobe Caslon
by Iain Bain, Newnham, Hertfordshire
Printed in Great Britain by
St Edmundsbury Press
Bury St Edmunds IP33 3TU

CONTENTS

ILLUSTRATIONS

Frontispiece: Reginald Hine
a portrait by Donald Brunt of Letchworth, *c.* 1930

Preface

Each time I walk along the street
I see the man I didn't meet
We didn't meet again today
Why did he choose to go away?

(After 'Antigonish' by William Hughes Mearns 1875-1965)

FOR MANY YEARS an imposing medieval banner hung on the wall of the main staircase at Willian Bury, the home of the lawyer and historian Reginald Hine on the outskirts of Letchworth Garden City in Hertfordshire. Woven in rich colours of crimson, blue and gold the five-foot tapestry depicts the churchman St. Vincent who was put to death in Spain during the fourth century and is now regarded as one of the great martyrs of early Christianity. In an ancient script above the saint's portrait are the words:

'To the glory of God and in memory of Reginald Hine.'

Not surprisingly, visitors were curious to know the story behind this banner and the man after whom the historian had apparently been named. It certainly intrigued Stella White when she arrived at the house in 1948 to begin work as nanny to Hine's grandchildren. One morning, as he came downstairs to join the family for breakfast, she ventured to ask about his ancestor. The response was a loud chortle of laughter. 'No! No dear girl! That's not an ancestor. It's for *me*! I've had the tapestry made specially, as a memorial to *me!*'

Throughout the years that Hine's bespoke tribute was on display he would perform a little ritual as he passed it on the stairs each morning. He would pause for a moment and offer a smart salute. 'Not today, St Vincent,' he would say. 'Not today.' Whether the remark was intended as a plea or a statement of defiance is not clear, but those who knew him would happily have given their eye-teeth to learn what he confided to the saint as he came down to breakfast on Maundy Thursday in April 1949. That was the day this flamboyant and popular man chose to end his life with a public act of self-destruction that many found hard to forgive. In front of dozens of travellers – including a party of children on a day-trip to London – he threw himself under the wheels of a steam train as it pulled into the station at nearby Hitchin, the medieval market town that had first brought him national recognition as an historian.

Hine had been a dominant figure in the cultural life of his county for forty years and the shock waves caused by his death were felt far beyond Hertfordshire. However, contemporary reports of the tragedy reveal a rather curious anomaly – the almost indecent haste with which the town laid its famous son to rest. Within forty-eight hours of his death a full inquest had been held and a verdict delivered. After a doctor had reported that Hine, who was 65, had been suffering from depression caused by overwork, the coroner recorded a verdict that he had killed himself while the balance of his mind was disturbed. The Vicar of Hitchin, despite being committed to a busy weekend of Easter worship, was asked to quickly arrange a memorial service in the parish church for Easter Tuesday. While that was in progress, Hine's remains were taken to London for cremation. The undertakers then brought the ashes back to Hitchin to be scattered that same afternoon amid the ruins of an ancient chapel on the outskirts of the town, as the historian had requested.

The memorial service itself was not the event his admirers had expected. No tributes were paid to the man or his achievements. One friend who was present described the service as cold and impersonal. Hine's name was mentioned only once. It seemed as if those who organised the valediction wanted to suppress all thought of the man. All of which begs a number of questions. Were they simply reflecting the community's shock, disapproval even, of the way Hine chose to end his life? Were there other reasons for his suicide? And, if so, was it agreed to hurry things along before further distressing facts came to light? Either way, more than three years were to pass before the people of Hitchin finally came round to giving their celebrated historian the civic recognition that many felt he deserved. Inevitably, one is forced to a conclusion that there may have been more behind this tragedy than was revealed at the time by the official inquiry.

* * *

Although I was growing up in Hine's town in 1949, I cannot recall his death or its immediate aftermath. As a schoolboy of fifteen, I had been away that week at an Easter scout camp and it was all over by the time I returned. Only later, during my early years in journalism with the *Hertfordshire Express*, did I begin to discover how much the man and his work were revered. Whenever I was called upon to write a feature involving some historical aspect of the county, my editor E.W. Hodson would immediately point me towards one or other of the weighty volumes that his old friend had written. Indeed, it was Hine who posthumously helped me to secure my first foothold at the B.B.C. when (in 1957) I plundered his much-acclaimed *Hitchin Worthies* to write a radio talk about Victorian England's legendary poaching twins, Albert and Ebenezer Fox, of Stevenage, whose centenary it was that year.

One day in 1959, shortly after leaving the *Express* to become a freelance writer, I was approached by a Quaker bookseller named Basil Donne-Smith. The Society of Friends – as the Quakers are known – had figured prominently in Hine's histories and Donne-Smith had been his close friend since the 1920s. An expert on antiquarian books and a campaigning president of the Booksellers' Association of Great Britain, he was a popular figure in the publishing world. He also owned Countryside Libraries Ltd., a network of private lending libraries run from his headquarters at the *Book House*, in Hitchin Market Place. It was there, just outside his shop that we bumped into each other one misty November afternoon. 'Ah! The very man! I've been meaning to mention this for some time, Richard. Now you're a free agent you really ought to get cracking on the biography of Reggie Hine, you know.'

It was the first time anyone had suggested that I might have the talent to write a book and I felt flattered that the proposal had come from a person of Donne-Smith's literary clout. However, his choice of subject did not excite me, as the expression on my face probably showed. Undaunted, he repeated the suggestion, adding almost conspiratorially: 'I mean it. You know, there is a *fascinating* story there, just waiting to be told.' I made a lukewarm promise to 'think about it,' but neither of us pursued the matter further. Probably he had realised that, with my heart set on a job at the B.B.C., a book about a recently deceased local historian came rather a long way down my list of priorities. Indeed, within a few months I had forgotten the conversation as I became immersed in a career in broadcasting that lasted for the next forty years. During that period Hine's books provided an occasional source of reference for my own literary efforts but I never read them for enjoyment, from cover to cover. For the man himself I felt no curiosity at all. However, Donne-Smith wasn't prepared to give up that easily. Having chosen me to be Hine's biographer he decided to wait until I had finished with the frenetic world of newsgathering and then try once more. So it was not until the new millennium, and some twenty years after his own death, that my Quaker mentor came to see me again.

The sequence of events leading up to his reappearance can be traced back to the day that a friend, Andrew Carmichael, sought my help in editing a set of notes that Hine had used in 1941 for a lecture entitled *Tales of Tilehouse Street*. Living in this picturesque part of old Hitchin Andrew was particularly keen to get the lecture re-published. In it, Hine takes a metaphorical stroll up the street, pausing outside the more interesting properties to discuss their history and to gossip about the characters that once lived there. Because his secretary had not been too successful in deciphering her employer's notoriously bad handwriting the re-constitution took us some time to complete. The job done we then hit upon the idea of re-creating the lecture on the 60th anniversary of its original war-time presentation, only this time with illustrations. I would deliver the talk while Andrew used a 1940s-period epidiascope to project a selection of ancient and modern photographs of Tilehouse Street.

The performance was arranged for a Sunday evening in July 2001 as the final event of the town's Arts Festival. The venue was the music room at Hitchin Priory, a former Carmelite Monastery where Hine once spent 'a year of Sundays' researching *The History of Hitchin* – the book that first won him national recognition. One evening, about a week before the event, I decided to set the scene for the evening by writing a short biography of the historian. It was well after midnight by the time I completed it and, once in bed, I fell asleep immediately. Just before dawn I was awaked by a dream; a very vivid dream in which the images appeared, unusually, in bright colour.

I was standing in the Market Place outside a double-fronted shop. In each window, and filling what seemed like acres of floor space inside, was a vast array of little bivouac tents of red, yellow and blue. Each one glowed brightly, as if lit from within by one of those portable gaslights that campers use. As I marvelled at this kaleidoscopic scene, the figure of a man appeared from the shadows at the back of the shop. Stepping neatly around the little tents he made his way towards me. When he emerged into the Market Place I realised that it was Basil Donne-Smith and he was carrying a book. He looked exactly as he had done forty years earlier when we last met; still beaming from behind his horn-rimmed spectacles; still wearing his snappy trilby hat, the maroon woollen scarf and dark grey overcoat. No words were exchanged. He simply smiled, waved the book aloft in a gesture of greeting, and passed by into the mist.

All this was easy enough to explain. The shop was *Millets*, purveyors of camping equipment and hiking gear, who had taken over the premises that were once Donne-Smith's *Book House*. What intrigued me was that, until that moment, I had totally forgotten about the man and the conversation we had back in the 1950s. Indeed, I cannot recall the two of us ever meeting again. Within a year of my joining the B.B.C. he had sold his business and retired to Somerset where he lived until his death in the 1980s. Now, here he was again, carrying a book that clearly symbolised this biography and waving it at me, not in greeting as I had first thought, but as a reminder to 'get cracking' on writing it. This time, his exhortation worked. As so often happens when one awakes in the small hours, my mind was alert and my thoughts crystal clear. One by one I began to recall Donne-Smith's remarks in as much detail as on the day that I first heard them. For more than an hour I lay awake thinking about what he had said, and by the time my reverie was interrupted by the first noisy soloist of the dawn chorus, the idea of writing Reginald Hine's biography seemed to be a very good one indeed.

The dispassionate reader will have a perfectly simple explanation for all this, of course. Having spent the previous evening dredging the backwaters of my memory for reminiscences, the retrieval system in my brain had continued working as I slept and had recalled the conversation with Donne-Smith in the form of a dream. However, you must forgive me if, like my subject, I adopt the more mystical approach and look upon this dream as a prophecy. For the deeper that I have delved into the life of this ethereal man, the more have I become convinced that all of this was pre-ordained; that it has been intended from the very beginning that one of my allotted tasks in this life was to write this book.

There was a time when I would have considered this minor brush with the surreal too embarrassing to mention. Certainly, I had no plans to commit it to print, until I discovered that the significance of dreams and other spiritual encounters was firmly embedded in Hine's psyche. Dreams were the subject of his first book in which he admits to being frequently tormented by demonic images; and his open-mindedness about the existence of a spirit world has continued down the family line to his grandchildren. Their recollections of moments verging on the paranormal, experienced during the days immediately following Hine's death, make interesting reading.

* * *

There is another factor that has drawn me closer to my subject than I could have imagined at the outset; the discovery of a number of similarities that we share. We were born just fifty years apart (he in 1883, I in 1933) and are both descended from the families of North Hertfordshire's yeoman farmers. At school we had a common dislike of and inaptitude for mathematics and the sciences. As young men we shared the same mischievous sense of humour that led us to play sometimes quite outrageous practical jokes upon those we considered vain and humourless. Although we both had the opportunity to sit a university entrance examination, we chose not to, opting instead for apprenticeships in our hometown. In 1901, Hine became an articled clerk with the Hitchin law firm of Hawkins & Co. In 1951, I was offered a similar post with Messrs Brignall, White & Orchard, a firm of solicitors in Stevenage but – to my parents' dismay – I turned it down at the last minute in favour of a journalistic apprenticeship with William Carling & Co., the publishers of our local newspaper.

There is also a marked similarity in the way our pastimes had a profound effect on the shaping and success of our careers. In the early 1900s, Hine's interest in local history became an all-consuming passion following his discovery of the wealth of historic documents in his employers' archives – a discovery that delayed his admission as a lawyer by many years. Half a century later, while serving my apprenticeship as a writer, I was learning through my great love of amateur theatre how best to deliver the spoken word. Through this I gained experience as a performer that proved invaluable when I found myself competing against two hundred other reporters for a job in broadcasting.

Personal experience also enabled me to understand the darker side of Hine's life. My daughters called them 'Dad's purple mists' when, at the end of a shift on the *Nine O'Clock News*, I would occasionally return home to spend the next two days slumped in a chair. Not wanting to go out; not wanting to communicate; drained of energy and snapping at anyone who tried to cheer me. When viewers asked how nervous I felt at the prospect of broadcasting live to millions of people every night I would tell them that I was so busy dealing with the technicalities of the broadcast that I did not have time to feel nervous. I believed that at the time but, quite clearly, I was wrong. The unpredictability of a live news broadcast may provide a wonderful 'buzz' when it is happening, but afterwards, when the adrenalin rush has subsided, it is a different matter. Fortunately for my patient family, the purple mists disappeared when I gave up the job that was causing them. Hine's problems were far worse. In *Confessions of An Un-Common Attorney* he writes candidly about his 'neurasthenia' – the archaic word that he uses to describe a nervous condition that began during childhood and haunted him on and off for the rest of his life. With the approach of old age, the condition became more serious, causing him make mis-judgements that turned him into something of a pariah among certain professional men in the town and led, ultimately, to his downfall.

I was also interested to discover how this amateur writer from a tiny and seemingly unremarkable corner of England managed to achieve such widespread recognition, simply by producing a handful of local histories more than half of which are little more than expensively bound pamphlets. After all, hundreds of men and women have produced similar well-crafted histories of their community but most are little known beyond their own areas. Yet, during the final decade of his life, Hine's fame as an author earned him an entry in *Who's Who* – Britain's definitive directory of influential people, in which names appear only by invitation.

There is also the question of how, in the recession-hit 1920s, an unknown author managed to persuade one of the country's top publishing houses to not only accept manuscripts of such limited general appeal, but use only the finest materials for their publication. This extravagance has certainly paid off because, nearly a century on, Hine's books are still sought by people all over the world, and a signed first edition in good condition can command a three-figure sum. In the 1970s when the antiquarian bookseller Eric Moore decided to re-print limited editions of *The History of Hitchin* and *Hitchin Worthies*, the public's response was such that he had to double the proposed print run. Even these re-prints are now selling at ten times their original price.

One disadvantage of researching a biography more than fifty years after the subject's death is that many of those who knew him are no longer with us. One advantage is that those who are still around have been prepared to speak far more frankly than they would have done in the 1960s, when Hine's immediate family, his widow and daughter, were still alive. The historian's three grandsons, who were very young when he died, have been eager to learn more about their famous Edwardian forebear, details of whose death were kept from them for many years. The oldest, Andrew McEwen, is just able to remember his grandfather. In an epilogue to this book, he reveals experiences suggesting that Hine's fascination with the paranormal may not have ended with his death.

The family has also put at my disposal papers and photographs that, for many years, have been locked away in a tin trunk, in the loft of Andrew's home near Cremona in Italy. Perhaps most important, by allowing me access to documents still held at the offices of the Hitchin law firm where Reginald Hine began his career, it has been possible at last to clarify the situation that led to the historian's suicide. Concern has been expressed that some of the revelations in this biography will lead people to look upon the man in a less favourable light. *The Ghosts of Reginald Hine* will certainly show him in a *new* light but it is one, I suggest, that will evoke sympathy more than criticism and that this wonderful and tragic eccentric will continue to be regarded as a gifted writer and sensitive student of humanity.

RICHARD WHITMORE
Hitchin, Hertfordshire
March 2007

[1]
Newnham: the Early Years

Reginald Leslie Hine was born on 25th September 1883, at Newnham Hall, near Baldock, in Hertfordshire. He was the third surviving son of Neville Hine, a tenant farmer, whose family had moved to East Anglia from the West Country in the late 18th century. They had settled first in Bedfordshire, where the historian's great-grandfather Thomas farmed before crossing the county border in 1831 to take on the 360-acre farm at Newnham. This subsequently passed to his son Joseph and then to Neville, the third and last generation of the family to farm there.

Newnham Hall is one of several farms in that area owned by the Farr family. Today, the acreage once farmed by the Hines has been absorbed into two adjoining farms also owned by the Farrs. Although the Hall itself is no longer a working farmhouse, its eye-catching frontage, walled gardens and fine brick outbuildings still dominate the road that leads out of the hamlet towards Ashwell. Newnham itself sits in a shallow valley amid prairie-like fields of wheat and barley on the last sweep of the Chiltern Hills before they level out into the rich flatlands of Cambridgeshire. When Thomas Hine took over the tenancy the property was known as Church Farm. In those days it looked far more like the working farms of early Victorian England; the house was somewhat smaller and shielded from the road by timber barns, stables for the working horses and a yard cluttered with machinery. Its grander-sounding name of Newnham Hall came later, after the original Elizabethan farmhouse had undergone a series of extensions and facelifts.

The Hines were God-fearing folk who had converted to Methodism from the Anglican church in the early 1800s. Both Thomas and Joseph became leading figures of the local Methodist circuit, supervising and helping to finance the building of a number of small chapels in Bedfordshire and Hertfordshire. In a twelve-page memorial published in *The Wesleyan-Methodist Magazine* in 1858 the writer recalls how before each harvest 'the master would call his labourers together in the fields and, before an ear of corn was cut, held a prayer-meeting under the canopy of Heaven; all unitedly acknowledging their dependence on the God both of seed-time and harvest, earnestly invoking His blessing.'

Throughout the summer, the labourers would rise at four a.m. to do an hour's work on their own small plots, tending vital garden produce for their families, before heading for the fields. Although horse-drawn cutters were already in use, much of the harvesting was still done by hand, using reaping hooks and scythes. The work was hot and back-breaking, the men working in lines of eight across the field, taking their time from the leading scythe-man – the 'Lord' as he was known – at the head of each line; their broad blades making an attractive ringing sound as they swished rhythmically through the corn. Along with Newham Manor, at the other end of the hamlet, the farm provided work for most families in the parish; so in the absence of a land-owning gentleman farmer the head of the Hine family became the equivalent of the local squire. As 'Mr Thomas' passed by on horseback on his daily rounds, the men doffed their caps and the women dipped in a curtsy.

The Hines enjoyed considerable prosperity during the first seventy-five years of their time at Newnham but, like most Victorian families, they suffered frequent bereavements caused by premature death. In 1856, shortly after succeeding his father at Newnham Hall, Thomas's son Joseph died at the age of thirty-five, forcing his wife to take on the running of the farm with her elderly father-in-law until his death, a little more than a year after that of his son. Reginald's father Neville was then aged eight and, because he was the oldest of Mrs Hine's three children, he was taken from school and educated at home so that he could learn the daily routine and skills of farm management as he grew up. In that way, he gained sufficient knowledge to enable him to take over from his mother when he came of age.

In 1874, Neville Hine married Eliza Taylor of Teddington in Gloucestershire. She bore him nine children, of whom two – a boy, Vernon, and a girl, Florence – died in infancy. In 1885 another daughter, Irene, died at the age of four, it is said after eating poisonous berries while playing in the fields. Of the six surviving children there were four sons, Hugh, Evelyn, Reginald and Eric, and two daughters, Ione and Dorothy. Because Eliza Hine was an Anglican the children were brought up to appreciate the convictions of both the Church of England and the Free Churches. So on Sundays the family went to Matins at Newnham's church of St Vincent and then to Evensong in the tiny Wesleyan Chapel that Reginald's great-grandfather had built shortly after arriving in Newnham. One clear sign that non-conformism remained the stronger element in the family's religious life emerges from the St Vincent's church registers which record only one of the Hine children – Dorothy the youngest – as having been baptised there.

The birth of Eliza Hine's ninth child left her in a delicate state, both mentally and physically. Her health continued to deteriorate until, in January 1892 at the age of forty three she died, leaving her children to be brought up by their father and the family's house-keeper Miss Afford, or 'Affie' as she was known to one and all. Reginald, who was eight at the time, left no personal record of this heart-breaking trauma which, on reflection, may well have been the point at which his own mental problems began. Only in one short passage in his book *Dreams and the Way of Dreams* is his sense of loss made acutely clear, when he recalls a recurrent dream in which his late mother appeared:

> I see her always the same. She sits in a chair by the fireside; and because she is cold and ill, she wears her furs to keep warm. I have my head and the side of my face pressed into the softness of the fur, while my brothers and sisters are lying on the hearthrug all around. It is always as it used to be. She tells me again the old nursery stories we loved so well, or some of the many folk-tales she had learned for our delight; and sometimes she will sing one of the songs of long ago, and then after that there will be the silence and the sadness that sweet music always brings; and the eyes will be growing heavy with sleep and, perhaps, with tears.

Eliza is also mentioned briefly in what turned out to be a

grimly prophetic paragraph in *Confessions of an Un-common Attorney*, when her son reflects upon his own nervous disorders:

> By this time I had grown ashamed of being a neurasthenic. 'You should remember,' scolded my doctor-brother (Hugh), 'that you come from a stubborn and healthy stock. Don't you know that it takes something terrific – something like a ten-ton lorry – to knock out a Hine?' But he had no panacea for an elusive malady derived, alas, from my mother.

Throughout the late Victorian era, while the children were still growing up, Neville Hine's farm continued to flourish. The rich crops of wheat and barley provided a comfortable income not just for the farmers, but for local brewers and millers as well. Just over the hill from Newnham, in the village of Ashwell, was the Fordham family's brewery and maltings. In the opposite direction, beside the River Ivel at Astwick, was James Bowman's water-powered flourmill that, in 1891, became one of the first rural mills in England to convert from traditional French millstones to steam-powered roller milling. The increased efficiency, coupled with Bowman's reputation for fair pricing, made Astwick one of the most popular flourmills in the district. With the threshing over, Neville Hine's men would be up before dawn to secure a place at the head of the long line of horse-drawn grain carts that queued patiently 'for two furlong or more' along the lane leading to the mill.

James Bowman's progressive approach laid the foundations of a company that became one of the most successful family mills in the country and one of the few that retained its independence into the twenty-first century. Their huge premises built near Hitchin Railway Station in 1901, became the focal point of the North Hertfordshire milling industry. When the company re-located to its present mill in Ickleford, the one at Hitchin was demolished to make way for a D.I.Y. store. Celebrating their centenary in 1957, Bowmans attributed their success to the fact that Hitchin is 'close to the finest, if not the best, wheat-growing areas in the country, the flour from which has proved eminently suitable for biscuit-making.' This soil quality was also spotted by the famous Carter's Seeds Company who, for several years at the beginning of the twentieth century, employed Neville Hine to grow experimental crops from the new strains of wheat and barley developed in their laboratories.

With agriculture and its associated industries dominating the local economy, farmers and millers played a more prominent role in public life than nowadays. Along with the Bowman brothers, Neville Hine became heavily involved in local government. He was among the first to serve on Hertfordshire County Council following its formation in 1889 and was eventually appointed a County Alderman. For more than thirty years he was Chairman of Hitchin Rural District Council, the local authority set up to administer the villages and hamlets of North Hertfordshire. As a Justice of the Peace he sat on the Baldock bench, where his powerful persona and huge walrus moustache are said to have had many defendants quaking in their boots. 'Those who met him for the first time were apt to be a little afraid of his rather formidable presence,' wrote his obituarist in the *Hertfordshire Express*. 'But they soon discovered that under those enormously shaggy and fierce eyebrows there lurked a pair of blue and twinkling eyes, and that his deep and magisterial voice was never anything but kind and merciful and witty in what it said.'

Neville's lawyer son left us no firm clues to indicate whether he shared this assessment of his father although, in *Confessions*, the general tone of his references to family life suggests that despite the early loss of their mother the children grew up in a very close and happy household. His respect for his father is reflected in a letter written in 1911 in which he says 'He has been the best father in the world to me.' Certainly, during a number of difficult years spent away at boarding school the young Reginald couldn't wait to get back to Newnham Hall.

His primary education was at a small school in Baldock bearing the rather grand name of The Grove House Academy. On his first day there the small boy was carried in, kicking and screaming, by a no-nonsense teacher after the coachman had been unable to coax him out of the family wagonette. For three

years, until old enough to go away to school, Reginald and brother
Evelyn received private tuition from the Vicar of Newnham, the
Reverend George Todd. Hine claims that much of their time at
the vicarage was spent gardening, while 'English composition' for
the twelve-year-old consisted of drafting sermons. These would
be culled from old books containing the oratory masterpieces of
long-dead churchmen and if the vicar liked the boy's interpretation
he would then pinch it, make a few adjustments, and deliver it as
his own the following Sunday. 'It was a pleasant existence,' Hine
recalls. 'If we were bored or felt over-taught, we had but to open
the window of the vicar's study when he was out of the room and
bolt across two meadows to our home. Often, in a fit of temper
over our truancies, our pedagogue would expel us on the Friday,
only to receive us back with open arms on Monday. We knew that
the fees were a useful addition to his stipend.'

Because the religious upbringing of the Hine siblings had
been divided between the Anglican and Free Churches, Reginald
decided never to commit himself to a single religion; preferring
to spend his adult life as 'a friend of all churches and a member
of none.' However, when recalling the Sundays of his childhood,
he seems to have derived most enjoyment from the time he spent
with the Methodists:

> Often, on Sunday evenings we would attend the little chapel
> that my great-grandfather had built and listen spellbound, not to
> sermons but to homely, village addresses from local preachers as
> rough and untutored as our blessed Saviour's disciples and apostles.
> How many elegant discourses from Doctors of Divinity, bishops
> and archbishops have gone over my head! But the simple words of
> John Wesley's men have a way of abiding in the heart.

One hazard facing those of Wesley's men who came to preach
at Newnham was Neville Hine's generous hospitality. Although,
as a J.P., he would not allow so much as a beerhouse to be opened
in Newnham there was no shortage of alcohol in his own house.
Visiting ministers were often invited to come early and join the
family for Sunday lunch and tea before taking Evening Service.

One's image of Victorian Methodists broadens considerably on reading the notes for a talk that Hine gave to a Wesleyan Methodist group in Letchworth Garden City during the 1930s, in which he spilled the beans about a certain Reverend Fred MacDonald:

> At Newnham we used to call him our most expensive guest. We said that he cost the family a thousand pounds because he taught my father to smoke. My father retaliated by teaching MacDonald to drink port, although to be frank he found him a surprisingly apt pupil. As a boy it was my business after lunch on Sunday to see the decanter circulated and I circulated it all the faster because I found that MacDonald's stories had a more convincing power and, indeed, almost a vintage flavour after six glasses of 1869. *Sub rosa* he told us things about the Wesleyans I had never dreamt of before; things you don't find in any official history of your church; witty, light-hearted, large-hearted things that made you love such people all the more.

The historian's renowned iconoclastic approach towards churchmen of all denominations probably stems from these boyhood observations; although, in later years, he seems to have had a twinge of guilt about the way he portrayed his tutor, Reverend Todd. Among the same set of papers that revealed the Fred Macdonald story was a photograph of Newnham's vicar, on the back of which Hine had written: 'Reverend George Todd, Vicar of Newnham. I wish I had treated him more worthily in my book.'

Reginald's first boarding school was Kent College, Canterbury. The thirteen-year-old doesn't appear to have been very happy there, partly because of the strong emphasis on mathematics, algebra and the sciences, which he hated. His literary skills continued to blossom, perhaps never more so than when, on behalf of his fellow pupils, he drafted a petition of protest to the headmaster that eventually brought about the dismissal of a brutal piano teacher inaptly named Mr Goodfellow:

Goodfellow, as his pupils with fear and trembling played their appointed pieces, would beat time with a ruler, and whenever we failed to keep time the ruler would beat down upon our wrists. If a false note were struck he would cuff the offender over the head, often with such violence as to sweep him off the piano-stool on to the floor. Once, in performing Mendelssohn's *Songs without Words (No. 19)* I hit the ground six times.

When he wanted to escape the harsher aspects of Victorian school life the boy found sanctuary in Canterbury Cathedral or, to be more precise, in the Dean's Lodge of Canterbury Cathedral. This had resulted from the first of what turned out to be an intriguing number of chance encounters that Hine had with older men as he made his way through life. On this occasion the meeting occurred in a Canterbury coin shop where Dean Francis Farrar, one of the best-known religious authors of the 19th century, stepped in to prevent the schoolboy being sold a dud coin. Within moments of rescuing him from the crooked numismatist the Dean had whisked the willing youth off on a conducted tour of the cathedral, after which he took him back to the deanery to give him tea and show him his own coin collection. Thereafter, 'tea at the deanery' became a regular treat. Sometimes he went alone, sometimes he was invited to bring some of his schoolmates. 'I was jealous when the others went,' Reginald wrote. 'Had it not been for me they might never have gone at all.'

Like many authors, Hine is at his finest when recalling the powerful spiritual experiences of his life. One the earliest occurred during an Evensong service in Canterbury Cathedral. Dean Farrar had arranged for him to sit in the choir, to hear what turned out to be the last sermon preached by the then Primate, Archbishop Edward Benson, shortly before his death in 1896:

> It was a sermon not to be forgotten, for the archbishop, without taking a text, spoke eloquently of the cathedral itself, and what it meant to England and the Christian faith. In the dim candlelight of the choir one was hardly aware of the congregation. The vast building, starting to life at the preacher's words, seemed rather to be filled with the listening spirits of the past. His one voice

– soaring, searching, penetrating – called up their multitudinous voices. The graves were opened. Master-masons, martyrs, monarchs, statesmen, churchmen, scholars, all came forth. To every claim he made as an ecclesiastic there was a cloud of witnesses, with a whispered 'Amen' from the common people buried in the nave. Above, in their storied windows, stood the saints in golden vesture arrayed and on every hand, carved and sculptured in wood and stone, there hovered a host of angels.

In the December of that same year, shortly before the Christmas holiday, Reginald contracted a severe form of pneumonia and was confined to the school sanatorium. At one point, the doctor became so worried about his condition that he called in a specialist who, after examining the sick boy, declared in a whisper loud enough for the patient to hear: 'This lad won't last long.' It was then standard treatment for pneumonia sufferers to be deprived of water. Convinced that he was more likely to die of thirst than anything else, young Hine was driven to creeping out of bed at night while the nurse was dozing and swallowing the contents of a water bottle used by the patients when they cleaned their teeth. Eventually the delirium subsided and, much to his relief, Reginald was allowed home. He spent the spring term convalescing in the comfort of Newnham Hall 'devouring good and bad literature, imbibing vintage 1863 port as prescribed and dreaming wildly at nights.'

In the autumn of 1898, Neville Hine transferred his son to a public school nearer to home, The Leys at Cambridge. Here, the fifteen-year-old had to follow in the illustrious wake of his eldest brother Hugh Fitz-Neville Hine, an outstanding scholar who went on to become a surgeon. So far as 'Hine R.L.' is concerned, school records show him doing rather less well academically. He obtained a 'Lower Certificate' (whatever that was) and a School Certificate Matriculation, that would have entitled him to sit the entrance examination for London University had he decided to take a degree.

As when at Canterbury, he admits finding it necessary to seek refuge yet again from the worst rigours of public school life. 'The brutality of the bullies, the hideous nightmare of the dormitories,' as he describes it. This time he found sanctuary in the private room of his English master, E. E. Kellett, 'a man who, being born with the soul of a poet, had sunk so low in the disfavour of God as to become a schoolmaster.' It was a friendship – in Hine's case, one would venture to suggest, a crush – that lasted for forty years, during which time the historian continued to submit his manuscripts to the long-retired master for correction. While most of us have fond memories of one particular teacher with whom we forged a special bond, few have written about them with quite such fervour as did Reginald Hine:

> When I recall my school days . . . I try to dwell only on the tranquil evenings in Mr Kellett's room, the deep and comfortable chairs, the soft glow of the fire, the buttered scones, the curtains shutting out the sight of the school, the rows upon rows of books with never a school-book amongst them, and my worthy preceptor himself, no longer a task-master but a poet, his pedagogue's face transfigured, his body, freed from its encumbering, awe-inspiring gown, moving rhythmically about the room as, from an unfailing memory, he recited hour after hour, some stirring Icelandic saga.

During the school holidays, meanwhile, the adolescent Hine was fast developing a fervour for the hobby that would eventually take over his life at the expense of all else. The history of his county. In his *Confessions*, tucked in among other examples of the blatant name-dropping that became a part of his style, there is a strong clue to how it all came about:

> Often, as a schoolboy, I would stroll across the fields from my home at Newnham Hall to the little village of Caldecote, to drink tea and play chess with the gentleman farmer Wickham Inskip and there sometimes I would find his nephew, now Viscount Caldecote and (from 1940-6) Lord Chief Justice of England. Whenever the nephew matched himself against his uncle, it left me free to curl up on the sofa and browse upon Inskip's Chauncy.

Chauncy - Sir Henry Chauncy – lived at Ardeley Bury near Stevenage and published his survey *The Historical Antiquities of Hertfordshire* in 1700. It is regarded as one of the classic topographical histories of an English county and was almost certainly the work that fired Hine's passion for local history and his determination to become Hertfordshire's Chauncy of the 20th century. Clearly, he lusted after Mr Inskip's copy of the work, even though it was not an original:

> It was the two-volume reprint in octavo of 1826, but the old gentleman prized it exceedingly and would never allow me to take it away. That being so I had to pore over its pages by his fireside, or in summer on the window-seat, and memorize all I could. I was twenty years of age before I was able to purchase a copy for myself, and by that time I knew some of the best passages by heart.

One would have thought that his love of history and the classics might have tempted Hine to sit the London University Matriculation entrance exam and try for a degree in these subjects, but he did not. He may have been deterred by his father who at that time was having to finance the education of three other sons and two daughters. Either way, in 1901 and having considered and rejected the idea of a career in teaching, Hine wrote home to tell his father ' … he could push me into anything else he cared.' That Easter, on his return to Newnham, he discovered that he had been pushed into the Law. An appointment had been made for him to attend an interview with W.O. Times, senior partner of the old Hitchin law firm of Hawkins & Co. for a position as articled clerk. So began an extraordinary relationship that enabled Hine to flourish as an historian, largely at the expense of his employer, for more than thirty years; thereby delaying his admission as a solicitor by almost the same length of time. All this is examined in a later chapter. For the present, it is worth recording that during the first fifteen years of his time with Hawkins & Co. the young man made the daily journey between his home and the firm's offices on a bicycle – a round trip of some twenty miles.

In the first decade of the Twentieth Century such journeys

were not at all unusual. With bicycles then outnumbering motor vehicles on the roads, there would have been no shortage of cycling companions for the young clerk as he pedalled along the winding country lane leading from Newnham to the Great North Road. He had a choice of two routes. The busier one took him south to Baldock where he turned off for Hitchin, passing the ancient hamlet of Willian where he would one day live. This way, he'd have found himself among many other cyclists and walkers as men and women journeyed in from the villages to the world's first purpose-built new town of Letchworth Garden City. By this time some factories were already up and running, offering exciting and hitherto undreamed-of employment opportunities to village families that, for centuries, had had to rely upon the vagaries of agriculture for their livelihood. Among the commuters were groups of young women who had been lucky enough to secure a job at the employee-friendly Spirella factory, making corsets and other fashionable foundation garments for the wasp-waisted women of Edwardian England. All enjoying the early stages of a changing economic pattern that would one day bring about the recession in Agriculture that sent many farmers to the wall – among them Neville Hine.

The other route was 'the country way,' along narrow lanes that took Hine past small farmsteads; crossing and re-crossing the county border with Bedfordshire until he reached the long straight road that leads from Stotfold to the outskirts of Hitchin. At its highest point, by the site of an old Roman fort on the Wilbury Hills, there is an impressive view of the market town and its satellite villages of Walsworth, St Ippolyts and Ickleford. Apart from being marred by a large block of industrial warehouses in the foreground and a distant line of giant pylons disappearing over the horizon, this outstanding piece of Hertfordshire landscape has changed very little. Hitchin's population may have trebled in the past century but the urban spread has been controlled and from this hilltop view the market town remains quite well concealed within its 'sleepy hollow' by generous clumps of trees. It is a view that Hine must have savoured hundreds of times as he reached the summit and then commenced the thrilling descent down the steep switchback of Wilbury Hills Road, under the railway bridge and on into the town.

During this daily journey, one imagines that the young writer was able to find inspiration for his first literary efforts. Early on a summer's morning, enjoying a solitary pedal past dew-damp pastures and fields of ripening corn, here was a chance to dream up story lines that would add a spot of colour and romance to the duller historical facts unearthed by his researches. Before his books, Hine had written essays, the first of which was about his home parish. *The Manor of Newnham* began life as a talk that the young man delivered to a gathering in the garden of Newnham Hall one sunny afternoon in August 1910. Thirty members of East Herts Archaeological Society, on an excursion to various historic sites in the area, had been invited to stop off at the Hall. 'There,' the local newspapers later reported, 'a picnic lunch, supplemented with liquid refreshment by Mr Neville Hine and served by his daughters, was partaken on the lawn; after which Mr Reginald Hine read a most delightful philosophic essay on the Manor of Newnham.'

The essay remains significant today because it shows how, from the outset, Hine had no compunction in allowing his imagination a free rein whenever he felt it necessary. In his opening remarks that day he declared:

> There is such a fever in the world to come upon the origin of things, and to account for all the pageant of man's life between his birth and his passing away that one is glad sometimes to throw one's mind very far back to a time beyond the reach of man's finding out, and there to re-create the past by the unhindered play of the imagination. Happily there are still some backwaters of life where this is possible – where one may give rein to one's fancy, and not be troubled by the intrusions and desecration of the learned; spaces of life beyond the contradiction of man's memory, or the pedantry and bareness of his early records.

The essay had been intended as Hine's 'audition piece' for membership of the Archaeological Society but the day proved to be something of a disaster for him. To understand why, one first needs to know something about those whom he was addressing.

Founded in 1898, East Herts Archaeological Society was then controlled by a small group of extremely dedicated amateur archaeologists and historians bent upon discovering new and exciting evidence of Hertfordshire's history. At weekends and holiday time 'excursions' were organised with almost military precision. For these, members wore the fashionable outdoor gear of the period, the gentlemen in Norfolk jackets, knee breeches and gaiters; the ladies in capes, high-neck starched blouses, full-length cycling skirts, lace-up boots and hats. After packing their sandwiches, their notebooks and pencils, their telescopes, shovels and magnifying glasses they set off for a chosen area to visit historic sites, to listen to talks and make copious notes and sketches. The more serious students would then write reports for publication in the Society's monthly magazine *Transactions*.

As with most amateur groups, many members joined as much for the day out as for the serious study of history; preferring to leave it to the devout few to organise events. In 1944, one of the early members reported:

> Some of the happiest days of our Edwardian childhood were spent
> when the E.H.A.S. went on leisurely pilgrimages through the
> gentle Hertfordshire countryside. Motors were few in those days
> and the main body of the caravan was a long line of wagonettes
> and governess-carts, upon whose flanks swarmed an auxiliary
> cavalry of dusty bicyclists. From vaguely Roman site to toy-
> inspired village church, from mouldering abbey wall to stoutly-
> built columbarium (in the vernacular 'pigeon and dove 'ouse') we
> went; at every halt, learned men read learned papers; and if, on
> cushioned pew or daisied mead, one dozed a little, it was with the
> comforting assurance that one would be able to read it all in the
> *Transactions*.

On the day they visited Newnham Hall, Hine's remarks about allowing free use of the imagination to enliven the 'pedantry and bareness' of historical records did not go down well with those senior members who were later to consider his application for membership. And any hopes that they may have been prepared to overlook the indiscretion were scuppered for good after they discovered what had happened to a most respected fellow member, Mr George Aylott.

During the refreshments following his talk, Hine fell into conversation with Mr Aylott and casually mentioned that a Roman burial site had reputedly been discovered in their garden many years earlier, turning up some interesting artifacts. Mr Aylott was the group's most compulsive digger and, with his appetite whetted, wanted to start a fresh excavation there and then. Hine pointed out that it would be rather rude to break away from the planned itinerary and suggested that if he cared to come back to the Hall on another day, he could begin work. Early the following morning Aylott was back, equipped with pegs, lines, pickaxe and shovel. Hine took him down to the lower garden, showed him the site where the burial ground was supposed to be and left him to it.

A couple of hours later the now perspiring Aylott came rushing back to the house triumphantly holding aloft an earthenware bottle that he confidently identified as Romano-British, circa 320 AD. Thanking his host profusely he carefully placed the treasure into his rucksack, tidied up the site and set off for home to write a report about his exciting discovery for the next edition of *Transactions*. Watching Aylott pedal off, Hine began to feel one of his familiar twinges of guilt. As he wrote later: 'One half of my life has been spent doing that which is evil and the other half in confessing it.' Thus, while George Aylott was at home writing his report for *Transactions*, Hine was penning one of his earliest 'confessions' in a letter to the society's secretary William Gerish.

In this he explained that he and his sister Ione had staged the whole incident as a practical joke. The 'Roman bottle' was in fact an Italian vinegar jar dated about 1840 that the two of them had buried a few hours before the E.H.A.S. party arrived. Mr Gerish was furious. There followed a vitriolic exchange of letters in which he berated Hine, not only for the 'reprehensible' practical joke but also for having had the gall to quote poetry, his *own* poetry at that, in a paper that was supposed to record the history of his manor. 'In his view', Hine recalled, 'that kind of embellished writing did not accord with the sober tradition of archaeological studies.' The upshot was that the joker was obliged to withdraw his application for membership and remained effectively blackballed from this august society for the next fifteen years. None of this little scandal reached the columns of the local papers, of course. Hine's 'delightful philosophic essay' as they described it was published in full and made to appear the highlight of the excursion. Having discovered what really happened that day it is not unreasonable to assume that the reports of the event had also been written by one Reginald L. Hine.

Many years later, after the founding fathers had passed on and when Hine had won respect as an historian, the archaeological society elected him their Vice President. During their Golden Jubilee celebrations in 1948 he delivered one of his most entertaining speeches, causing great hilarity when he finally confessed to the prank that got him blackballed. However, the questions first raised by the society's elders in 1910, suggesting Hine could be distorting history with his colourful literary embellishments, continue to be debated to the present day.

In his early photographs, the historian comes across as rather superior; in appearance, not unlike a young Oscar Wilde. A bit of a couch potato, perhaps, who hated exercising anything more than his writing hand for fear that it might cause him to break into a sweat. In fact, the reverse was the case. School records show that, despite his illnesses and his abhorrence of the rougher aspects of public school life, he was quite an accomplished 'second team' sportsman, representing The Leys at both cricket and lacrosse. After leaving school he took up cricket, golf and shooting and had a fierce service at tennis; the kind of weekend activities for which his daily bicycle ride to work and back would have kept him extremely fit. Mrs Ina Roberts, of the Bowman milling family, remembered Hine at the tennis parties held at their home at Rook Tree House, Stotfold: 'Tennis was such an important social event for country people during the first part of the 20th century. Most of the larger houses had a grass court, so there were parties almost every Saturday afternoon throughout the summer. The hosts always provided a wonderful spread of cakes and little sandwiches, with tea and lemonade served in only the best glasses and china. Reggie was one of the keenest players.'

It is for prowess on the cricket field that Hine the sportsman is best remembered. He played regularly at the Ashwell village team and for Hawkins & Co. in their annual match against the rival law firm, Longmores of Hertford. In the early 1900s he became a valued member of Hitchin First XI when the club's ground was situated along the old London Road on land now occupied by the houses of Coach Drive and Lister Avenue. Spectators have recalled seeing him whack a number of sixes clean over the line of trees that surrounded the field. However, cricket was not the only attraction that drew the young law clerk to this fashionable neck of the woods. Here, too, was the home a certain Miss Florence Pyman, the future Mrs Reginald Hine.

[2]

Marriage and Dreams

AMONG A HANDFUL of large houses gracing the southern outskirts of Hitchin at the end of the 19th century was a large Georgian residence called The Oaks. The property has since been divided into two dwellings and now stands in Oaks Close among a cul-de-sac of houses that were built much later in the original garden. Florence Pyman lived at The Oaks between 1896 and 1906. She belonged to a very wealthy family of Yorkshire ship owners and it is unlikely she would ever have moved to Hitchin were it not for a tragedy that befell them.

Florence's grandfather was George Pyman (1822-1900), founder of the Pyman Shipping Group which, prior to the First World War, was one of the largest family shipping empires in Britain. Between 1865 and 1930 its various companies commissioned the building of some seventy-five new ships, mainly tramp steamers. Much of the family's fortune was made from exporting coal. George claimed to have started work at the age of ten helping to crew a fishing smack, and before he was twenty-one he had obtained his master's ticket. His first ship was an old Whitby brig in which he had a part share and which he worked until he could afford to buy his first vessel outright. In 1850 he left the sea and went into business, first as a ship's chandler in West Hartlepool and then as a broker and fitter. As his firm expanded, so George began to commission and operate more vessels, including a screw-propeller steamer, which he named after himself, and others that he named *Lizzie English* – after his wife – and *Raithwaite Hall* after the mansion just outside Whitby where the couple raised their large family.

Of George and Lizzie's nine children seven were sons, a fact that became instrumental in the expansion of the Pyman Shipping Line during the second half of the 19th Century. As his boys completed their education and training so their father was able to spread his interests further afield, to Cardiff, Newcastle and Hull, where he founded new steamship companies for them to run. Two brothers – Fred and Frank – were sent down to London to launch the ship-broking business Pyman Bros. of Bishopsgate and it was Frank Pyman's family who came to Hitchin to live in 1896.

Frank was the youngest of George Pyman's boys and is remembered as an exceptional classics scholar. He read law at Trinity College, Cambridge, graduating in 1878 and subsequently obtained an M.A. It was at Cambridge that a fellow undergraduate, Walter Lee, of Sedgeley Hall, Manchester, introduced his sister, also named Florence, to Frank. Their father, Henry Lee, was head of the large Manchester cotton firm of Tootal, Broadhurst & Lee. Florence Lee and Frank were married three years later, in 1881, moving down to London when Frank joined his brother at the Bishopsgate company. Over the next ten years the couple spent their time between the capital and the family estates in Lancashire and Yorkshire. They produced five sons and the one daughter, who was christened Florence after her mother.

By this time, George Pyman's success in the shipping industry had made him one of the most influential men in the North East, where his record of public service ran on almost identical lines to that of Alderman Neville Hine, down south in Hertfordshire. At various times George was Mayor of Hartlepool, a councillor for the North Riding and a Justice of the Peace for Durham County. In 1864 he was made the local Belgian Consul – a recognition often awarded to successful businessmen by countries with whom they had generated strong trading links – and was subsequently decorated by the Belgian government for his services. On a visit to West Hartlepool in 1890 the Duke of Clarence was quoted as saying: 'The name of George Pyman is one of the most prominent names connected with the great shipping industry of the country.'

George's youngest son, meanwhile, had begun an active political career as a supporter of Gladstone's Liberal Party. Throughout the 1880s Frank Pyman became more and more involved with the Liberal cause, helping in election campaigns and acting as Private Secretary to Lord Rosebery when Rosebery stood for the newly-formed London County Council in 1887. A year or two later,

Frank was adopted as the Gladstonian candidate for his home constituency of Whitby to fight the General Election of 1892. Although the *Times* reported that his speeches 'made a distinct impression on the electors' they were not persuasive enough to win him the seat. It was a defeat that had dreadful repercussions for the loser.

Frank had suffered from health problems on an off for several years and had had to spend a number of periods convalescing at health resorts abroad. On this occasion, the strain of the election campaign and the shock of his defeat proved too much. He suffered a severe nervous breakdown from which he never properly recovered and for the rest of his life he was plagued by recurring bouts of 'deep melancholia.' In those less-enlightened days chronic depression was a condition which, like epilepsy, was still classified as a form of insanity. As a result, this sensitive and talented classical scholar was certified 'insane' and at the age of forty-one was committed to a mental institution, where he spent the remainder of his long life.

It was a terrible time for his young family. Mrs Pyman – who had just given birth to their sixth child – had to apply to the 'Master in Lunacy' for a protection order under which Frank's considerable fortune was placed in a trust fund. It was shortly after this that she purchased The Oaks and brought her family to Hitchin. Why she should have chosen this little-known market town where she had no family connections is unclear. It could have been to do with the education of her younger boys or that there was a period during the early days of her husband's illness when he was being treated at the Three Counties Asylum at Arlesey, just across the county border in Bedfordshire. In which case Hitchin, three miles away, would then have been the closest town.

Old hospital records preserved from Victorian times failed to reveal a Francis Pyman among the patients. However, it is an interesting coincidence that in 1896, the year that Frank's family moved to Hitchin, the asylum began treating its first group of private patients prior to opening a private wing. As things turned out, the money generated annually by the Pyman trust fund ensured that, despite the shortcomings in knowledge about his illness, Frank was able to receive the best possible treatment and care for the remainder of his life. He was eventually admitted to The Priory at Roehampton, one of the foremost private psychiatric hospitals in the country, which is still functioning today in beautiful grounds adjoining Richmond Park.

The turn of the century brought another year of sadness and change for the family. At The Oaks in August 1900 Frank and Florence's youngest child, Cyril was struck down with gastric fever and died at the age of eight. In December of the same year the founder of the Pyman dynasty, grandfather George, died at the age of seventy-eight. His large fortune was divided equally between his many children but because of Frank's 'insanity' the part due to him had to be treated differently. His share was instead divided equally between his own children, the four surviving sons and his daughter Florence. However, because women were still some way from full emancipation, the law did not allow the little girl to inherit her share as a lump sum. Instead, the money due to her was invested in another trust fund from which she was permitted to receive only the interest that her inheritance earned.

When Reginald Hine began his articles with Hawkins & Co. in 1901 Florence would have been twelve years old; an attractive lass with striking red hair and the inevitable strong will that comes from being the only girl in a house full of older brothers. While the boys were away at school, Florence was educated at home by a governess, a Miss Dawson, whose widowed mother ran a drapery store in Hitchin Market Place. So from this it seems likely that the young couple's attraction to one another did not develop until towards the end of the Pyman's ten-year stay in Hitchin, by which time Florence would have been approaching her eighteenth birthday.

Similarly, *how* they met can now only be a matter of conjecture. Their grandson Andrew McEwen recalled that in their early days together the couple shared a great love of music, poetry and languages – particularly Italian, a country where they later spent their honeymoon and where Florence subsequently took many holidays. They then liked to play the piano and sing together, so it could have been that they met at one of the musical *soirées* that were so popular in Edwardian times. Or was Reg in rather good form one summer afternoon when Florence and her mother took a stroll across London Road to the cricket field to watch the Saturday afternoon match? More prosaically, it could simply have been some legal matter that took Mrs Pyman and her daughter to the Portmill Lane offices of Hawkins & Co. on a day when this personable young man happened to be the clerk on duty behind the front counter.

However it was that the couple came to meet, their mutual attraction continued to strengthen after Mrs Pyman gave up The Oaks and returned to London, having purchased a house in Lancaster Road, Swiss Cottage. Their love also survived the two years that Florence was away at a finishing school in Paris. In searching for a bond that brought them together it is natural to wonder whether – in the light of her father's illness – Florence's love for Reginald was strengthened by her compassion for his own bouts of anxiety and melancholia. Andrew McEwen did not think so: 'Nothing that my grandmother said makes me think she was aware of his mental problems so early in their relationship. What seems more likely is that he was attractive to her because he was very different to other men, because he was entertaining and told good stories.'

Yet, even in his twenties, Hine's outwardly extrovert character hid a much-troubled mind. Just how troubled was revealed many years later in a strange and morbid letter discovered among his personal effects. Written in 1911, the year before their marriage, it is addressed to Florence and signed *Guido*, an Italian pet name that Hine used during their courtship. Written on five pages of blue notepaper it also contains a will in which he leaves instructions on the dispersal of his few personal effects and where he would like to be buried. At the time, the couple's wedding day was seven months away but the letter shows that plans were already well advanced and they knew they would be living at Ashwell, the village just over the hill from Newnham:

'My dearest Girl,
From a child I have had as you know over me the shadow of

an early death. This used to trouble me and throw gloom and melancholy over my spirit. But now all this has passed and I believe now whenever my end shall come I shall be unafraid and shall not grieve because it is in the flow of my life that I am called away. I have firm faith in the love of the All-Father and shall yield myself a child into his hands – nor have I any doubt that my soul shall perish with my body. It will awake out of the dream of life to the glorious dawn of the invisible world – and I shall die assured that there one day our spirits shall be reunited.

'I used to pray with heart in agony that I might not be taken away in the midst of my days – I no longer pray that prayer. Since you dear heart of mine have come into my life I have known fullness of joy and the love between us has been so great that I feel that even though it must cease so soon I have known already the best that life can offer . . . My will dearest girl leaves all the little I possess to you absolutely because I want to feel that the books and old fashioned things I loved through my youth will be about you still and bring often to you the memory of the lad to whom you gave your love.'

Writing several years before he began his great love affair with Hitchin and the old ruined chapel at Minsden where his ashes are scattered, Hine asks:

'Let me be buried in Newnham Churchyard wherever you shall choose – it has been a desire of mine to lie awhile in the midst of my books. (By this he means his book collection) If I die at Newnham let them place my body in the study until it shall be rendered to the earth. If at Ashwell in the study there upstairs. My spirit will linger I think where I have been most happy.'

He then makes a careful list of his few possessions – his watch and chain, his tennis racquet, his cricket gear, his 'old, well-loved bicycle,' some paintings and books and asks for them to be distributed to specific members of his family. At this time his first two literary efforts, the essay *Anima Celtica* and the book *Dreams and the Way of Dreams* were still in manuscript form and he asks

Florence to do her best to make sure that they are published. The final page of the letter is the formal declaration of the will, witnessed by two of his fellow clerks at Hawkins & Co., and dated 7th September 1911. His parting words to Florence are:

> 'And all the rest dear heart is to be yours and greatest of all the memory of the wonderful love that we have known together and the sure and certain hope of reunion with you in the life to come. Farewell – my spirit shall be very near to comfort you as you read this when I am dead – it will watch over you throughout your days lovingly and tenderly until the day when you too shall say goodbye to earth to join me.'

As events turned out, of course, Florence Hine did not read this letter until nearly forty years later, when it was discovered among her husband's papers following his suicide. The effect upon her of reading for the first time this poignant echo of love from their youth does not really bear thinking about. Even a century later, the outsider feels a sense of guilt for daring to eavesdrop upon such privacy.

Reginald and Florence were married in London on 11th April 1912, in the chapel of New College, Hampstead, not far from the bride's Swiss Cottage home. The Hines being Methodists and the Pymans Congregationalists the marriage took the form of a Free Church ceremony. Although the wedding certificate records the bride's father as 'Frank Pyman, ship owner' it appears that the poor man was considered too ill even to be at the wedding of his only daughter. For it is his wife's signature that gives witness to the ceremony, along with those of Neville Hine and Onslow Times who, one presumes, was best man. Mr Times – if he noticed it at all – must have decided to turn a blind eye to the fact that Hine had audaciously given his profession as 'solicitor' when, in all honesty, he should have written 'solicitor's clerk.' He describes himself similarly on his passport; two early examples of a disregard for legal etiquette that would ultimately lead to his downfall.

* * *

Ashwell End, where the couple spent the first five years of their marriage, is a splendidly preserved Jacobean farmhouse, situated in an isolated spot three-quarters of a mile across the fields from Ashwell village itself. When the Hines became tenants in 1912 it had just been saved from ruin by a local philanthropist, Mrs Wolverley Fordham of the brewery family, who employed the distinguished garden architect Sir Walter Tapper, (1861-1935) to oversee restoration work. As a result, all the original features of this fine 16th-century yeoman farmer's house were saved.

The couple must have been delighted to have it as their first home. Their contentment is clearly reflected in a handful of family snapshots taken in the garden during their first summer there. It could well have been these images of his wife that inspired Hine's dedication to her in *Dreams and the Way of Dreams*, which was published the year after their marriage:

TO FLORENCE.
To you who are in name and soul a flower,
For whom the world a garden fair doth seem,
I give these blooms from my most secret bower:
Roses of reverie – lilies of dream.

Completed as he was approaching his thirtieth birthday, the book would be well nigh impossible to place with a publisher nowadays. Like *Anima Celtica*, his 1912 essay on the humour and character of the Irish people, it was very dated even at the time it came out. The genre is reminiscent of Victorian *belle-lettres*, when aspiring authors with no particular qualifications could get away with writing about scientific or spiritual matters so long as their style appeared eloquent and learned. Another essential ingredient was a liberal sprinkling of quotations in Latin, Greek or French from well-known writers of the past; a touch much favoured by Mr Hine throughout his career.

Naïve though his theories now may seem, *Dreams* remains important in that it provides a key to the enigma of the historian's private world. Knowing now of his fascination with all matters psychic, a number of clues about his personality emerge through accounts of the 'extravagant and violent' dreams that he experienced throughout much of his adulthood; dreams that he allowed to spill over into his waking hours. 'It is not good for one's peace of mind to dwell overlong thinking on these unknown plays in our dreams,' he wrote. But dwell he did. His grandson, Andrew McEwen, explained the historian's strange reveries this way:

> My grandfather was convinced that there was something of value in this vagabondage of the subconscious, something that lay beyond the scope of psychological analysis, but also beyond human interpretation. 'The best of our dreams are born out of a mystery, and they carry away their own meaning with them into the mystery where they return,' he wrote. The book set out to show that our nocturnal visions have suffered from over-analysis by science and over-dismissal by the worlds of philosophy and religion, with the result that few have dared to venture into this field for fear of looking foolish. My grandfather was one of those gentle souls, a person who preferred 'to dwell within mysteries without striving to probe them to their depth.' What interested him was not run-of-the-mill dreams, but rather those that are experienced as reality, so extraordinarily vivid that we emerge from them in the conviction that we were not asleep at the time.

For this reason our dreamer-historian had no time for the views of Sigmund Freud (1856-1939) the founder of psychoanalysis whose theories on dreams (like those of Carl Jung slightly later) were the subject of world-wide debate at that time. Instead, Hine chose to dwell in a romantic fairy-tale world, relying upon quotations from philosophers of old to garnish his theories. Even in nightmares, Hine's pretensions towards highbrow classical literature came well to the fore. Here is part of his description of a recurrent 'Falling Dream' when the lift in which he is travelling gives way and plunges downwards:

> I was reading out of a folio volume one of the dialogues of Plato; it was the *Symposium*, and I was just come to the finest part of it, where Socrates concludes the discussions by a criticism of the

preceding speeches, and by unfolding in his perfect way the true nature of Love ... As soon as I knew there was no hope all the fear went out of me, and I was quite indifferent to the thought of coming death. I knew that it would be a great while before the lift came to the bottom; so I determined at any rate to finish the oration of Socrates before I died. I was soon under the spell of this, and forgetful of all things in life but the charm that was in the winged words of the master and the divine excellence of the spirit of Love. And it was as I lingered over the closing words that the end came. There was a terrible crash, as of rending timber; the book was hurled away out of my hand, and as I reeled across the floor of the lift, the sides of it fell inwards upon me.

Not all his dreams were that fanciful. Others were triggered by more predictable traits - human rivalry, bullies from his schooldays and his own mortality. One particularly lively nightmare followed a visit to an exhibition of medieval armour at Hertford House. In this, our historian found himself clad in chain mail and doing battle with an ancient knight. After his assailant had fallen fatally wounded Hine bent over him and lifted the vizor. 'The sight well-nigh slew me,' he writes. 'I tremble now as I think of the awful heart-rending horror that came to me. It was *my own face* that I looked down on; my own self that lay dying ... I knew that with the ebbing of his life, mine too must pass away. And so it was.'

Eventually, there came a time when the ferocity of these nocturnal encounters forced him to seek medical advice. Some of this is detailed in *Confessions of an Un-Common Attorney*, along with graphic accounts of more vivid dreams that – even in middle age – showed no signs of abating. 'I dream as extravagantly and violently as ever,' he reported. 'I wish it were not so, for sometimes in the hours of dark I alarm my household with moans and groans and gibberish not of this world, and find myself still fighting on the floor ... Most of the beings I meet in the middle of the night are hideous and hostile. By day I try to fill my mind with gracious and peaceful thoughts. At night I am delivered up to a horde of demons.'

By the outbreak of the Great War in 1914, the historian was

convinced that his mind was beginning to crack and sought the help of a number of local doctors. Among these was the superintendent of the Three Counties Asylum at Arlesey who he asked, somewhat melodramatically, to reserve a room for him. However, all those who examined Hine seem to have been convinced that the young man was suffering from little more than bouts of anxiety brought about by nervous exhaustion. So, in lieu of bromide or valium, they prescribed that good old-fashioned standby of early 20th-century medicine, a daily glass of port.

Despite his nervous problems, Hine decided he would volunteer for war service and reported to the Army Recruitment Centre at Bedford for a medical examination. He was turned down; the official reason being that his childhood bouts of pneumonia had left him with lung damage. However, the senior medical officer seemed far more interested in the strange contents of Hine's book and proceeded to take him to task for 'deliberately disregarding' the theories of Freud. Hine admits that, on the army doctor's instructions, he finally yielded and bought a copy of Freud's *The Interpretation of Dreams*. In this the psychoanalyst sets out his theories about dreams revealing the 'socially unacceptable desires' that men and women have to keep suppressed during their waking life. Such was Hine's shock at what he read that, thirty years later in his *Confessions*, he was still seething about it:

> I purchased the recommended volume for thirteen shillings; read it intently in the train, turning the leaves with prurient fascination and increasing disgust every evening, and on the seventh day consumed it with fire. There are some books so vile that you ought not to sell them, still less should you give them away. I disliked dropping thirteen shillings. I loathed reading libidinous things that would be fixed in my memory forever. Merely to pitch such a book into the flames was not enough. Tearing out the pages with savage deliberation one by one, I made sure that this hypersexually-minded scientist, this Caliban of the enchanted island of our dreams, should have a lingering death.

Would it be unkind to suggest that another reason for Hine's dislike of Freud's theories was that some of them came a little too close to home? One thinks in particular of another nightmare in which – armed with his shotgun – the historian endeavours to fight off hordes of malevolent demons: 'What exasperates me above all in my struggles with these evil spirits is that my gun will not go off. I pull at the trigger desperately but there is no discharge.' He believed the nightmare – that 'impotence' as he described it – stemmed from the guilt he felt after shooting a barn owl on his father's farm at Newnham. No doubt Herr Freud would have had other ideas, offering one of those 'libidinous' explanations that had caused his book to be consigned to the flames.

Hopefully, any anxieties that her husband may have had in this department would have been allayed fairly soon afterwards when Florence became pregnant, giving birth in 1915 to their daughter, Felicity; an only child and a source of great joy to the couple. Yet it seems that even with his own daughter Hine could not resist the temptation to probe into the little girl's dream world. Many years later, Felicity was to tell her own children how, when she was small, their grandfather would sit by her bed waiting for her to wake and, as soon as her eyes opened, would demand an account of her latest dream, which he promptly wrote down in his notebook.

With her husband now making even longer bicycle journeys into Hitchin and returning late each evening Florence was left to her own devices for much of the time. She enjoyed helping with the annotation and preparation of his manuscripts and, like most young mothers, took part in village activities. She developed a particularly close friendship with her landlady Mrs Wolverley Fordham, who introduced her to the then fast-growing Girl Guide movement. By the 1930s guiding was a major feature in the lives of both women; Mrs Fordham having become the Hertfordshire County Commissioner and Florence the District Commissioner for Hitchin.

To some of the sturdy agricultural folk of Ashwell, 'that writer fellow' was regarded as a bit of an oddball. Mrs Bessie Wallace whose family, the Sales, have farmed in that parish since the 17th century, was seven years old when the Hines moved to Ashwell

End. She well remembered accompanying her mother when she called on Florence Hine to introduce herself. 'To this day I can still see Mrs Hine quite vividly. She was so charming and lively and we all admired her lovely red hair. Reggie was rather different. He had some very nice brothers but we were a bit dubious about him. My father thought there was something very odd there; even as a young man he always had a wild look in his eyes.'

Curiously, Ashwell's excellent little museum holds no record of Hine's links with the village. Neither is there any mention of him in an illustrated feature on Ashwell End that appeared in *Country Life* magazine in 1949 shortly before his death. By that time the house had become better known as the home of another historian who had taken over the tenancy shortly after the Hines left. John and Janet Beresford, who lived in West London with their four children decided to rent the old farmhouse as a country retreat for which Mrs Fordham charged them only £30 a year. Beresford was a senior civil servant in the Treasury, a job he did not particularly enjoy. Rather like Hine he derived more pleasure from his spare time occupations. These included editing personal accounts of our social history. The most famous of these is *The Diary of a Country Parson*, which came to be published only because of the Beresford's move to Ashwell.

The Reverend James Woodforde, (1740-1803) held livings first in his native Somerset and then in Norfolk. For more than forty years he kept a diary in which he recorded a detailed picture of daily life in rural 18th-century England. For more than a century the seventy-two volumes of Woodforde's manuscripts were passed down through various members of the family until they came into the possession of Dr R.E.H. Woodforde of Ashwell. The doctor, who had opened his surgery in the village in 1900, was probably the first to recognise their historical significance.

One day in the early 1920s, when he was treating John Beresford for a bout of scarlet fever, he mentioned the diaries to his patient and asked whether he would be interested in editing them for publication. Beresford read them and immediately accepted the offer, with the result that, between 1925 and 1931 a five-volume abridged edition of the diaries was published by Oxford University

Press. These were followed by a further selection, published as a single volume in 1935. Such is the interest in Woodforde's writings that there is today a Parson Woodforde Society whose members are dedicated to publishing the *complete* diary, the original of which is now held in the Bodleian Library at Oxford. In his *Confessions*, (pp.192-3) Hine makes the contentious claim that Dr Woodforde had first offered *him* the job of editing the diaries, as a therapy to help cope with his mental problems, but he had turned it down:

'What you really need,' said that sensible village doctor, 'is some literary or historical work that will not merely occupy but fascinate your mind for at least five years.' Then he walked across the surgery and opened a large safe. 'Here,' he said, handing over a pile of eighteenth-century manuscript, 'is the diary of an ancestor of mine – a parson at Weston Longville in Norfolk. Read it, and, if you like it well enough, then edit it. It will please our family; and it would do you a world of good.'

Sorry doctor,' I broke in. 'if I did anything of that kind it would be a history of Hitchin. But just now I can't string three sentences together, and can't make sense of anything I read.'

'It is a pity,' he observed, putting the diary away; and 'What a pity!' I echoed ruefully in after years when John Beresford, who succeeded me in the Jacobean house at Ashwell End, made a name for himself as an editor, and for Parson Woodforde as a eighteenth-century character, out of that self-same manuscript.'

Some members of the Parson Woodforde Society are sceptical about the historian's claim and doubt that Hine ever saw the diaries. If he had, they say, it is unlikely that he would have referred to them in the singular as 'the diary' and 'a pile of 18th-century manuscript' when the originals consist of seventy-two separate diaries, each one individually bound.

One of the reasons the Beresfords decided to move to Ashwell in 1918 was because Janet had become worried that the increasing number of Zeppelin bombing raids on the capital was threatening the safety of their children. So there is a sad irony in the fact that twenty-two years later, in October 1940, her husband should be killed by an enemy bomb while on fire watching duty on the roof of a government building in Whitehall. John Beresford was fifty-two years old and reputedly the first fatal casualty of the Blitz. After his death, Janet gave up their London home to live permanently in the Hertfordshire retreat that they and their children loved so much. She remained a prominent and popular figure in village life until she left *Ashwell End* in 1973, shortly before her death. The affection with which this family is remembered in the village is perhaps best reflected by the fact that the Jacobean farmhouse that they enjoyed for more than fifty years has been given a new name. It is called *Beresfords*.

* * *

Hine's other somewhat controversial link with Ashwell concerns the memorial tapestry that he commissioned for himself. It was made by Percy Sheldrick, a renowned master weaver who was born in the village and later worked for the leading tapestry manufacturers Morris & Co., at their Merton Abbey factory. A shy and deeply religious man, Percy died in 1979 in his ninetieth year but his remarkable needlework can now be found all over the world in homes and churches, including Westminster Abbey and St Paul's Cathedral. Some of the finest is on display in Ashwell's parish church of St Mary, where he was verger for many years.

There is a story of how, one Sunday afternoon in 1969, Queen Elizabeth the Queen Mother, an expert needlewoman in her own right, spotted Percy's work during a private visit to the church and was so impressed that she immediately asked to meet him. Percy, a bachelor, was in the middle of washing up after lunch when a breathless churchwarden arrived to let him know who was on her way to see him. The royal guest spent the remainder of her visit talking embroidery with Percy in the sitting room of his tiny bungalow in Back Street. 'What a craftsman!' she exclaimed as she emerged. 'I've never seen such needlework!'

Sheldrick and Hine had first met in the late 1930s when Percy called at the lawyer's office in a state of great agitation to seek advice on a difficult family dispute. He then unwittingly guaranteed himself a place in Hine's *Confessions* by requesting that the two of them pray together before discussing the case. So, side by side, they knelt in silence for a few moments on the Persian carpet in front of Hine's desk. 'What followed was another instance of the efficacy of prayer,' the historian wrote. 'One by one the apparently insuperable difficulties and dissensions disappeared. The letters that had been so bitter became surprisingly friendly. The opposing parties came together to compose their differences. The irreconcilables were reconciled. The family feud was ended.'

The next time that Percy called on his lawyer, he brought with him a book of tapestry designs and invited Hine to choose a pattern that he liked. He explained that he had a month's holiday due to him and wished to spend it making his solicitor a tapestry as a gift. Hine says he was deeply moved by this offer and chose a medieval pattern from the famous Unicorn tapestries at the Cluny Museum. Curiously, he makes no mention of the fact that he exploited Sheldrick's generous offer by getting him to make the Reginald Hine Memorial Tapestry, even though – at the time he was writing his *Confessions* – it was already hanging above the staircase in his home.

* * *

When the author moved to Hitchin in 1917, his family's links with Newnham and Ashwell were already entering their last phase. One by one, Neville Hine's six surviving children had begun to move away; one son went to London, another to Ireland. His two daughters Ione and Dorothy emigrated to South Africa, having by a remarkable coincidence both married wealthy South African students whom they had met while the young men were up at Cambridge.

Ione's wedding on 30th August 1913 was probably the last big family celebration to take place in Newnham. She chose to have an Anglican marriage service for which the little church of St. Vincent was decorated as never before with palm leaves, evergreens, grasses and white flowers – a joint effort between the Hines' neighbour, Miss Cooper from the Manor, and Richard Ward, the gardener at Newnham Hall. Brother Reginald composed a special five-verse hymn for the service and every cottage along the route to the church was decorated with bunting. As the couple emerged they found that the villagers had formed a long guard of honour to shower them with confetti.

Among the hundred guests was a strong contingent from Cambridge University Rowing Club, the bridgeroom, Jonathan Ayliff, being their champion sculler. The previous year he had been Cambridge's 'spare man' for the memorable 1912 Boat Race, which was started during a half-gale and is now on record as the only race during in which *both* boats sank. It had to be re-run on the Sunday, April Fool's Day, when Oxford won by six lengths. One can feel some sympathy for Ayliff's best man, S.E. Swan, who had been the Cambridge stroke and, by the time of the wedding, must surely have been thoroughly tired of the requests to recount his version of the disaster.

An indication of the Hine family's standing in the local community at that time is provided by the rather obsequious paragraph that ended the *Letchworth Citizen's* report of the wedding:

> Succeeding (Hine) generations have, by their noble characters and charitableness, greatly endeared themselves to the villagers, so that it is questionable whether they honoured the bride on Saturday or her father the most. Certain it is that 'Miss Ione' has made herself by her charm and innumerable acts of kindness, a warm corner in the hearts of all those who live in and around Newnham.

After a short honeymoon in England, the couple left by ship for South Africa. Ione spent the rest of her life there, living in Grahamstown where her husband was a partner in the family law practice. They had two daughters and Ione died in 1975 at the grand age of ninety. Her sister Dorothy, a bridesmaid at the wedding, later married Jon Ayliffe's friend Robert Matterson and they, too, went to live in South Africa. The Mattersons also had two daughters who, unhappily, were still children when their mother died suddenly in 1923 at the early age of thirty three.

Hosting Ione's wedding day was Neville Hine's last big 'hurrah' before the Great War and economic recession sent his business into a steady decline from which he was unable to effect a recovery. The elders among other farming families in this corner of North Hertfordshire have recalled how they became worried about the way their neighbour was allowing his farm to take second place to his unpaid career in local government. As the war ended Alderman Hine was approaching his seventies and with none of his sons willing or able to take over, he struggled on until – in common with many other tenant farmers at that time – he found himself beset by financial problems. In the early 1920s his affairs were put into the hands of an official receiver and the farm's management was eventually taken over by its owners, the Farr family, descendants of whom are still there today.

The old man and his devoted housekeeper 'Affie' spent their retirement living frugally in one of the eight new council houses that were built on Newnham Green in 1921, just a short distance down the road from the Hall. Alderman Hine had become a tenant of Hitchin Rural District Council, the local authority he had led as Chairman for more than 30 years. In view of his long record of public service and the fact that his farm had provided employment for so many in the community, one would have thought that the villagers might have considered him to be as deserving of help as anyone else when he fell upon hard times. But in the recession-stricken years of the early 1920s many farm workers and their families were still living in terrible hovels and, with new council houses at such a premium, those Newnham families with young children felt they should have had first call on each house as it was completed.

Consequently, when the key to Number 8 was handed to Alderman Hine, the air around The Green could have been cut with a knife. Things were not improved when the new tenant rather tactlessly allowed his son Evelyn to live there until he and Affie were ready to move in. The ill feeling was further aggravated by allegations that some of the fittings the council installed in the Alderman's house were of a far higher quality than those in the other seven. All of which resulted in the Hine family's association

53

with Newnham ending on a slightly sour note.

Mrs Sheila Rosendale, the last of the original residents still living on The Green, was one year old when her father – a local gamekeeper – was allocated a house. Her strongest childhood image of 'Mr Neville' was seeing him at the Sunday service in the little Wesleyan chapel that now serves as Newnham's village hall. As if to preserve a family tradition remembered from his childhood, he would sit facing the rest of the congregation in the chair specially installed for his grandfather, Thomas Hine, when he founded the chapel in the early 1830s.

Neville Hine – hopefully unaware of the sniping and gossip going on behind his back – remained at Number 8 for the last ten years of his life; just long enough for him to see his son publish *The History of Hitchin*. Happily, when he died at the age of eighty-two, his life was recalled in a positive and affectionate obituary notice that contained many warm tributes to his forty years of public service. The old farmer had outlived his wife Eliza by forty years. As he was buried beside her in St Vincent's churchyard on a frosty January morning in 1931, the Hine family's link with Newnham came to an end. It had lasted just one hundred years.

[3]
'My Father-in-the-Law'

IF THE GREAT WAR contributed to the financial ruin of
Neville Hine, the toll it exacted from the Pyman family was far
greater. In one year – 1917 – no fewer than nine of their merchant
ships were lost at sea through enemy action and by the time the
Armistice was signed Florence Hine had lost two more of her
four surviving brothers. Major Colin Pyman, DSO and Bar, and
Lieutenant Ronald 'Bon' Pyman were both killed in action on the
Western Front. A third brother, Geoffrey, despite taking part in
some of the worst fighting of the war, returned safely having been
awarded the Military Cross and a Distinguished Service Order.

In contrast to the financial misfortunes of Hine's father, most
of Frank Pyman's wealth survived the years of war and recession,
thanks largely to the foresight of his brothers. Just before hostilities
broke out, they decided to dispose of their shipping fleet and had
managed to sell off a number of vessels while prices were still
high. They sensed correctly that the coal industry upon which the
fleet depended would be going into decline; a decline that was
later accelerated by the general strikes of 1921 and 1926. So the
companies on which their fortune had been built were gradually
closed down or sold as the younger members of the family found
new interests and careers. Florence's eldest brother, Frank Pyman
junior, became a prominent chemist and Fellow of the Royal
Society, winning several awards for his pioneering work in the
development of chemotherapy.

With their trust fund still strong the family were able to
continue the lifestyle they had enjoyed before Frank Pyman senior
became ill. Not long after Reginald and Florence's wedding in
1912, Mrs Pyman sold her Swiss Cottage home and bought a large
town house in the Cromwell Road, from where the journeys to
Roehampton, to visit her husband at the Priory Asylum were much
easier. Their daughter's security was already assured by the regular
income from her grandfather's legacy; a blessing appreciated as

much by Hine, who had inherited little if anything from his side of the family. It was due almost entirely to Pyman wealth that the historian, earning the modest wage of a solicitor's clerk, was able to continue living in the comfortable style that he had enjoyed at Newnham Hall during the prosperous years of his father's farm.

Having moved to Hitchin from Ashwell End in 1917, Reginald, Florence and their daughter lived for the next twelve years at Riddy Shott in Wymondley Road. This unusual cottage-style house belonged to Hine's employer, Onslow Times. If it looks as though it may have inadvertently slipped down the hill from Letchworth, it is because it was designed by Geoffrey Lucas, who was one of the six principal architects responsible for the design of the Garden City. When the Hines occupied the house it stood in a six-acre orchard and had unimpeded views across the Ashbrook valley to the villages of St Ippolyts and Preston. The best view of all was from the window in Hine's study, which was one of two rooms built into the roof. It was here that he wrote most of the one thousand pages of *The History of Hitchin*. He often worked by candlelight long into the night, writing and re-writing each page in longhand with a simple steel-nibbed pen and black ink – not a quill as has been romantically claimed. His insomnia and bad dreams meant that he was often awake and back at work in his study by four a.m., reading or writing until it was time for breakfast.

After breakfast the historian would take his daily ten-minute walk across Windmill Hill and down to the offices of Hawkins & Co. in Portmill Lane. This famous hilltop vista of Hitchin has changed somewhat since those days. The unappealing blocks of flats, the tarmac spread of the St Mary's Square car park and the hideous array of aerials and satellite dishes on the roof of the 1950s telephone exchange were still to come. In 1917 the scene from the hilltop was a myriad of tiny slate roofs and smoking chimney pots that made up what were then known as the Queen Street slums. Here, divided from the rest of the town by the River Hiz, were what Hine described as 'a squalid quarrelsome underworld of little yards' – Chapman's Yard, Gascoigne's Yard, Webb's Yard, Thorpe's Yard, Peahen Yard and Barnard's Yard. In each huddled a score of crumbling cottages, some over three hundred years old. They were similar to the one-up-one-down hovels inhabited by farm workers but packed much closer together. Most had earth floors; their 'garden' was a small central yard containing a couple of stinking earth closets and a single cold water tap that the families had to share. Dotted among these typhoid-ridden tenements were thirteen pubs and several slaughterhouses.

The people who lived there were a tough lot. They had to be to survive. The men laboured on the railway or at Russell's leather dressing works; their womenfolk and children plaited straw to be sold on Market Day to plait dealers supplying the Luton hat factories. There was also seasonal work on the lavender fields or picking vast amounts of rose hips, dandelions and other wild plants to sell for a few shillings to William Ransom's distillery. It was a neighbourhood where policemen patrolled in pairs and into which nobody who was not a resident liked to venture after dark. As a young reporter on the *Hertfordshire Express* Reg Cannon's work took him into the slums more times than he cared to remember, particularly during the years of the Great War. Of more than 350 Hitchin men wasted in that conflict, many came from the Queen Street community and it was usually Reg who was sent there to interview the bereaved families. He has left us this unforgettable description of one such visit:

Dickens himself would hardly have believed what I walked into. There were three generations in this house, in two rooms. The telegram delivered that morning brought news of the death of the father of six or so children who were there. They were the third generation and were seated on broken boxes and chairs round a bed on which newspapers were spread. They were having their tea. There was no table – the bed had to do for that. I got my facts and the inevitable photograph from the fly-blown frame and was given every help by the widow, but it was an experience I have never forgotten. The bed that served as the tea-table was occupied by the father of the soldier who had been killed. He, too, was dead, but there seemed nowhere else to put the body so it was left in the bed and tea was served around it. Do you wonder why I think that the clearance of those slums was the finest and most humane thing done in Hitchin during my lifetime?

Because of the war, the town council's plans to demolish the slums had to be delayed until 1925. During the following four years this large area of medieval Hitchin was razed to the ground, opening up the whole eastern end of the great parish church. Lawns were laid stretching down to the river, which had been widened and edged with ornamental brickwork. A waterfall was added and two bridges were built, leading pedestrians up sets of granite steps onto the new St Mary's Square. On the central flight of these steps are engraved words commemorating the demolition of 174 cottages and the re-housing of 637 inhabitants elsewhere in the community. Costing just over £83,000 it was the most sweeping single face-lift in the town's history and it all took place while Hine was completing *The History of Hitchin.* An inspiring story on which to end his book one might have thought; and yet it is dismissed in just four words, in a chronology of local events:

1927-1929 Queen Street slums demolished.

Perhaps he considered it too topical to be 'history.' Even so, it seems a surprising omission, not least because one of the men who masterminded the project was his employer, the prodigious Onslow Times; the man without whose encouragement Hine would never have produced the books that established him as an author and historian.

* * *

When Gilbert and Sullivan's popular light opera *The Mikado* opened at the Savoy Theatre in 1885 one reviewer was quick to point out that, although set in Japan, the show was really a thinly-veiled satire of Victorian England's institutions and the characters who ran them. One such character is Pooh-Bah – The Lord High Everything Else – whose positions in The Town of Titipu include First Lord of the Treasury, Lord Chief Justice, Commander-in-

Chief, Lord High Admiral, Master of the Buckhounds, Groom of the Back Stairs, Archbishop and Lord Mayor. Such was this character's impact that the word 'Pooh-Bah' soon became a part of our vocabulary, describing – not always in a kind way – someone who has managed to land all the plum jobs.

For some fifty years, between 1880 and the early 1930s, William Onslow Times was the Pooh-Bah of Hitchin – and much of the rest of North Hertfordshire come to that. Born in 1851, the year of The Great Exhibition, Times possessed those qualities of Christian zeal and boundless energy that were the hallmark of many eminent Victorians. A dynamic personality whose obituary notice was, the *Hertfordshire Express* observed, 'one of the most remarkable records of public and private service ever published, not only in this town and county but in England itself.'

The second son of Charles Times, a solicitor and coroner for the Hitchin Division, Onslow was born at No 23 Tilehouse Street, shortly before his family moved to a larger house in the town's wide and fashionable main street of Bancroft. He was educated at Bishops Stortford College where he obtained an exhibition to St John's College, Cambridge. However, his father's failing health compelled him to abandon his university plans and join the family law practice as an articled clerk. When Charles died in 1872 the young Times' articles had still not expired so a friend, John Hawkins, took him into the firm of Hawkins & Co. where he completed his articles and was admitted as a solicitor a year later. Thus began an astonishing career in public service during which Times held single-handed a range of public appointments that these days would provide lucrative careers for at least half-a-dozen senior civil servants and goodness knows how many staff.

In 1876, at the age of twenty-five, he became the youngest county court registrar in England and at the time of his retirement had control of five different courts with jurisdiction over seven counties. He was also Clerk to the three separate magistrates' courts of Hitchin, Stevenage and Welwyn. In local government, he was Clerk to the authorities of Hitchin from 1873 to 1925 and Stevenage from 1879 to 1921. He oversaw their change from Local Boards to Urban District Councils and all subsequent improvements to amenities in the two towns; from drainage and water supplies to hospitals, welfare services and housing.

In the early 1880s the Crown Estates decided to sell off an ancient Royal prerogative under which they had been entitled to levy 'pickage and stallage' tolls on the market town. The Hitchin Board authorised their young clerk to go to the London auction to bid for the toll rights. When these were knocked down to him for £4,000 and the auctioneer inquired the name of the purchaser, Times' reply 'The Town of Hitchin, Sir' was greeted with loud cheers from the two hundred people present.

On top of all this, the lawyer managed to find time to serve on the boards of several local companies and to become a leading lay figure throughout the Diocese of St Albans. In his home parish of St Mary's he managed the church school for sixty years and was vicar's warden for more than thirty.

In a bid to keep young men in touch with the church after they became too old for Sunday School, he founded and led the Hitchin Church Adult Class, where he taught almost every Sunday afternoon until his death. He also edited the parish magazine, presided over the local debating society and lectured authoritatively on the history of his native town.

Perhaps one of the reasons Times was able to undertake so much work was because he never married. However, he was a strong family man, much admired by his nephews and nieces, to whom he was known as 'Uncle Willie.' To the community at large he was 'Onslow Times' and to his employees he was 'The Master.' However, within a short time of joining Hawkins and Co. Reginald Hine had invented his own name for his mentor. He called him 'my father-in-the-law' – word play that assumes a rather deeper significance when placed alongside the observations of those who knew and worked with the two men. For, before long, it seemed that Hine had become one of the Times family.

Just why such a close friendship developed between Onslow and his young clerk invites a number of theories. The most plausible of these is that the bachelor Times, much taken with this tall and elegant eighteen-year-old, saw him as the son he would have liked to have had. A 'son-in-the-law' that he could groom to succeed him when he retired and who might one day be head of the law firm. At the time of Hine's interview in 1901 Onslow was already fifty years old. One can well imagine him listening as this confident youngster aired his already extensive knowledge of Roman Law and the history of Hertfordshire and thinking that here was someone whose intellect could be put to good use for the benefit both of Hawkins & Co. and the town in general.

So it was that Hine found himself enjoying the sort of blissful existence that most young and struggling academics can only dream of. He was articled to the district's most distinguished lawyer who allowed him a free rein to indulge in his time-consuming passion for historical research. When shown the wealth of ancient documents crammed into the cellars and attic rooms of Hawkins & Co.'s Jacobean building, the young man could hardly believe his luck:

> My good fortune lay in the fact that, for thirty-five years, first under articles, then as assistant solicitor, I was attached to one of the oldest firms in the land, that of Messrs. Hawkins and Co. of Hitchin. But the best of my days were spent half doing my duty in that state of life into which it had *not* pleased God to call me and, by the good nature of my master and father-in-the-law, William Onslow Times, devoting the other half to the discovery of manuscripts for the history of a Royal and Ancient Manor. For the sort of life I had in mind to follow, the conditions were ideal.

In other words, although Hine was prepared to accept a full day's wage as 'a budding conveyancer,' his employers were getting only half-a-day's work out of him as, with The Master's approval, he slipped away from his desk to plunder the firm's archives. The bookseller Basil Donne-Smith likened Hine's cosy situation to that of a mediaeval scholar, 'securely ensconced in the entourage of some great household and freed from many of the chores of workaday existence.' Hine brazenly admits:

> I never tired of spying into the history of the foremost Hertfordshire families. Once you were able to prise open the

narrow wooden boxes –so reminiscent of coffins – there, when
the dust had died away, there it all was, from the cradle to the
grave; extracts of baptism from the parish register, pedigree
notes and achievements of arms on vellum, the first stilted essays
submitted to the family tutor and preserved by doting parents,
college reports of a later date, bills for 'sumptuous clothings and
banquettings' incurred at Oxford or Cambridge, the resettlement
of the estate at twenty-one, batches of love letters, letters of a more
scandalous character from the black sheep of the family, which
'family skeletons' if brought to the light of day, had to be tactfully
reinterred, myself retaining a funny-bone just for remembrance,
settlements upon mistresses, maintenance of natural children,
abductions, seductions, blackmailings, breaches of promise, letters
in dishonourable exile from the uttermost parts of the earth, first at
frequent, then at infrequent intervals, fading at last into silence.

In those days Hawkins were still managing the estates of
Hitchin Priory, which had been the home of the local squirearchy,
the Delmé-Radcliffe family, since Henry VIII's Dissolution of the
Monasteries in 1538. One of the historian's greatest coups was his
re-discovery of the original deed of surrender that the Carmelite
Friars had had to sign under pressure from the king's agents
in 1539. He came across it by accident one Sunday afternoon
while working in the Priory's muniments room. Sifting through
documents in an old Spanish chest he happened to touch the
release mechanism of a secret drawer. The parchment deed, which
had not been seen for more than a century, was revealed in perfect
condition and with the seal of the friars still intact. No doubt it
was Times who had persuaded the Delmé-Radcliffes to allow
Hine to spend his 'year of Sundays' in their home, examining
the wealth of documents, books and artifacts in their library and
muniments room. No doubt it was Times' influence that later
gained his clerk access to numerous other historic homes and
archives across the county.

If Onslow looked upon Hine as an adoptive son, Hine saw
Onslow increasingly as a new and welcome father figure who
– unlike his own rather prosaic father – shared his enthusiasm

for the romance and characters from History and the Classics. Despite a difference of more than thirty years in their ages, they became close friends and almost constant companions. At weekends, they played golf together at Royston or Letchworth, where Onslow was both captain and president during the forty years that he played there. It was Onslow who was Reginald's best man at his wedding in 1912; Onslow who became godfather to his daughter in 1915 and Onslow who provided him with a house when he brought his family from Ashwell to Hitchin in 1917.

For much of his life, Times lived in a large house along the Bedford Road in Hitchin. A casual researcher going through Hine's papers could be forgiven for thinking that *he* lived there as well, so many of his notes and jottings are written on Onslow's personal notepaper bearing the Bedford Road address. It must have seemed as much to Fred Warren, a clerk with Hawkins & Co. for many years. When he was the office junior one of Fred's chores was to sort through the morning post and then jump onto his bicycle to take any letters addressed to Mr Times or Mr Hine up to Onslow's house. There he would find the couple enjoying breakfast – 'always toast, marmalade and coffee from a silver pot.' Describing this ritual to Eric Moore in 1983, Fred said he would have to wait until as many as fifty letters 'in much danger of being opened with the marmalade knife' had been read. Hasty notes were then scribbled on the backs of envelopes for him to decipher later back at the office. The two men seem to have spent most evenings together as well. Long after everyone else at Hawkins & Co. had gone home, they would still be at the office preparing for the rest of Onslow's busy week:

> Often at midnight when at last we had finished with the law, he would rehearse two or three speeches to be delivered on the morrow, and sketch out his sermons for the following Sunday. It was the privilege or at any rate the duty of an articled clerk to listen, to criticize, to provide embellishing touches out of a more general reading; and in this way my early training as a sermon-maker under the Revd George Todd came in useful.

It is not clear whether all these late nights and early mornings were the cause or the result of the breakdown in the Hines' marriage. But after only five years the partnership between Florence and Reg (as she always called him) was no longer the intimate and joyful affair that it had seemed to be at the outset.

PORT MILL, HITCHIN
Drawing by Samuel Lucas

1. Newnham Hall, birthplace of Reginald Hine, as it is today.

2. A postcard of 1906, showing part of the garden of Newnham Hall. To the left are seen the walls of a quadrangle of barns which until the 1960s stood on the lawn seen in the present day view of the Hall.

3. A Methodist Church rally at Newnham Hall in 1897 (from an old booklet). Reginald Hine is the taller of the two boys in the front row.

4. Alderman Neville Hine J.P

5. Ione Hine, the historian's sister.

6. St Vincent's Church, Newnham.

7. The grave of Hine's parents, Neville and Eliza, in Newnham Churchyard.

8. The Hine memorial tapestry in St Vincent's.

9. Ashwell End, the Jacobean farmhouse where Reginald and Florence lived between 1912 and 1917. It has since been renamed Beresfords.

10 - 11. The Hines at Ashwell End during the first summer of their marriage.

12. The Oaks in London Road, Hitchin, in 1900 when it was home of the Pyman family.

13. A family group in the garden. Florence is standing and her mother, Florence Lee, seated left. Next to her, with the cigarette, is the oldest son Frank. Their coachman and landau can be seen in the background.

14. In this 1914 snapshot Florence Hine is standing between her husband and two brothers, Colin and Ronald 'Bon' Pyman, both of whom were killed in action on the Western Front.

15. The grave of Florence Hine's parents and her eight-year-old brother Cyril in Hitchin cemetery.

16. Florence Hine's parents, Frank Pyman Senior and Florence Lee, at the time of their engagement.

17. A romantic *carte-de-visite* taken on honeymoon in France in 1881.

18. Hitchin Cricket Club First XI and officers in 1907. *Standing* (L to R): R. Passingham, Dr H. Grellet, G. Roberts, R.C. Grellet, R.L. Hine, E. Leete, N. Goddard and Major Amos. *Seated* (L to R): F. R. Shillitoe, H. Williams and H.E.S. Salusbury Hughes. *On the grass* (L to R): G. Cooper, H. Pearce, S. Brown and the Revd Mandel Jones.

19. Hine's first studio portrait, taken by Beatrice Cundy of Mayfair *c*. 1908.

20. Florence in her Red Cross uniform during the Great War.

[4]
'Amicus Amicorum'

THE SELFISH DEMANDS that authorship makes upon a marriage can provide a pretty stern test of that partnership's stability. Many writers try to resolve the problem by adhering to a strict working timetable, but when the project becomes an obsession all of that goes out of the window. This happened to Hine when his move from Ashwell End to Riddy Shott brought him within much easier reach of the mass of archive material requiring his attention. Also, he was now less than an hour's journey by rail from his favourite places of research and relaxation: the Public Record Office, the British Museum, the antiquarian bookshops and the London lecture halls, where he could hear and occasionally meet some of the literary figures of his day. Not surprisingly he was rarely at home and, when he was, he was upstairs in his study.

Commenting in later life about various marital disputes that he had been called upon to resolve during his legal career the historian wrote: 'The hardest thing to read is not handwriting, but human beings; and of human beings the hardest to make out are those united contradictions husband and wife.' This somewhat bitter view of wedlock is, one would suspect, based as much on personal experience as on the cases he dealt with. For the joyful intimacy that had prevailed in the early years of Reg and Florence's marriage had by now been replaced by a rather chilly formal relationship in which the only human bond holding them together was their daughter. After Felicity's birth, it appears, Florence had pulled up the drawbridge and for the rest of their time together the couple conducted a celibate marriage, sleeping in separate rooms and allowing each other freedom to pursue their different interests.

This distancing is particularly noticeable in accounts of Hine's public life. Among all the reports covering his appearances at events across the county not one could be found at which the presence of *Mrs* Reginald Hine was also recorded. However, it is unlikely that the public noticed this. Because the couple had so many different interests it would have been assumed that each was far too busy to attend the other's events as well. At Hitchin Girls' Grammar School, where Felicity was a pupil, hardly a year went by when either Reg or Florence was not invited to speak to the girls or to judge a competition. Even in 1923, several years before *The History of Hitchin* was published, the school magazine was reporting:

> The school spent an enjoyable afternoon on Monday March 27, listening to Mr Hine's lecture on old Hitchin entitled *A Walk Down Bancroft*. Many of the fine old buildings in that well-known thoroughfare took on a totally different aspect after their past history had been so vividly told … On Thursday December 14th Mrs Hine lectured to us on the League of Nations, which was especially interesting as she and her husband had attended, at Geneva, the recent conference of League members. She introduced the delegates to us and explained how the League had already averted war between several countries.

Having lost two brothers in the Great War, and, as a Red Cross volunteer, seen examples of the appalling injuries suffered, Florence devoted much of her time to promoting the League's pacifist objectives. Largely through her influence, the branch at her daughter's school had more than 150 members who held numerous fund-raising projects in aid of the League's campaigns during the inter-war years. Despite their distancing, Florence continued to give her husband tremendous support as he approached the end of his long quest to complete *The History of Hitchin*. As editorial assistant she undertook all the annotation and indexing that is such an important part of the book and played a major part in enrolling subscribers to help finance its publication. The couple were greatly helped by Richenda Payne (later Dr Richenda Scott) an enthusiastic history student from the Grammar School who went on to become an historian in her own right and a close family friend.

The antiquarian bookseller Eric Moore once recalled that local history was a subject that rarely matched up to the well-known dictum of Herman Melville, author of *Moby Dick*, that 'to produce a mighty book, you must choose a mighty theme.' In the 1920s, as now, major publishers were wary about investing money in material of such limited general appeal. So when, in 1927, Hine approached the fast-growing publishing firm of George Allen & Unwin with his manuscript, he was told that they would only be prepared to publish it 'on commission.' In other words, he would have to pay the entire cost of production himself, after which Allen & Unwin would sell the book for him, taking a percentage on the sales. Philip Unwin, who had just started with the firm, later recalled the episode in his memoir *The Publishing Unwins*:

> Needless to say I shall never forget my first author. This was the
> late Reginald Hine, a literary solicitor, who produced a stupendous
> history of Hitchin in two volumes. He was a tremendous extrovert
> and though of Quaker inclination he had a poetic flow of speech
> calculated to win over everyone.

The same qualities that enabled Hine to persuade his Quaker friends and others in the county to stump up a sum of money which – because of his ambitious plans – was far more than that normally needed to produce a book. 'My petition is that the good people of Hitchin should make it go,' he wrote in his appeal brochure, and they did not let him down.

Although he had steadfastly refused to nail his colours to the mast of any specific religion Hine had by middle life come closer to the Religious Society of Friends than any other sect. In his dealings with them he referred to himself as *Amicus Amicorum* – Friend of the Friends. The part these good people played in the growth of Hitchin fills more than a hundred pages of his history. Richly illustrated with sketches by the Quaker artist Samuel Lucas this section won warm approval from the Friends nationally and was later published separately under the title *A Mirror for the Society of Friends*.

Quakers also feature in *Hitchin Worthies*, the third book of

Hine's trilogy, which contains entertaining pen portraits of a number of the market town's benefactors. Although the historian has described Hitchin as 'A Quaker Town,' the Friends made up but a small fraction of the population. Even at the peak of their influence, there were never more than two hundred living in the parish. Yet, whether trading as wool merchants, brewers, chemists or bankers, they were much respected for their honesty and fair dealing. Their popularity led to some quietly making a fortune, much of which they immediately put back into the community. Barclays Bank in the High Street was once the Quaker bank of Sharples, Tuke, Lucas and Seebohm, two of whose directors played a major part in founding the town's present education system. The donation to the community of Joseph Sharples' old house The Woodlands, in Bancroft, led to the founding of the Boys' Grammar School in 1889. Similarly, Frederic Seebohm, living just across the street at The Hermitage, donated land on Windmill Hill for the Girls' Grammar School, which was opened in 1908. He also gave most of his seven-acre garden to the townspeople to enable them to create Hermitage Road. Of all the old Quaker families, those of Exton, Latchmore, Lucas, Ransom and Seebohm are still remembered today through the schools, streets, buildings and open spaces that are named in their honour.

It was the Ransom and Seebohm families whose money guaranteed publication of *The History of Hitchin*. With modesty befitting their faith, they asked that they should not be singled out for special recognition. Consequently, they are almost lost among the one thousand subscribers who purchased a copy in advance and whose names fill nearly thirty pages at the back of Volume One. In the book's acknowledgements, gratitude is expressed simply to 'the two gentlemen of Hitchin whose generosity has made it possible to offer this volume for half the price at which it would otherwise have been published'.

Although he had succeeded in raising the necessary capital, there still remained the baffling question of how this virtually unknown author managed to sell his parochial tome to an international publishing house the size of George Allen & Unwin Ltd. To understand this, one has first to appreciate the strength of

Hine's lofty belief in the quality of his work. Nowhere is this better illustrated than by an extraordinary incident that occurred in 1911 when he was trying to place his first full-length book *Dreams and the Way of Dreams* with a publisher. He submitted the manuscript to J.M. Dent & Sons of Letchworth Garden City who passed it on to one of their readers, a noted Irish poet and literary critic named Darrell Figgis, for assessment.

Figgis reported that, while he quite liked the subject matter and its presentation, he felt that Hine had tried to copy the style of the 17th-century religious writer Sir Thomas Browne – '*and does not quite succeed.*' Because of Figgis's lukewarm response Dent decided not to accept the manuscript. Now, the rejection slip is a disappointment that most authors have to address at some time in their career. When one arrives the would-be author can only shrug it off, take on board any constructive comments the publisher may have to offer and then set about preparing the manuscript for submission to another publishing house. Unless you happen to be Reginald L. Hine.

Incensed by the rejection, the young man headed straight for the publishers' offices and demanded to see Hugh Dent, the person who had returned his manuscript. When told of Figgis's report, Hine insisted upon knowing *exactly* what the reader had said, and when Dent unwisely allowed him to see the letter, he exploded in fury. Having noted the letterhead bearing Figgis's private address in Hampstead Garden Suburb, Hine stormed out of the office and headed straight for the railway station. The story continues in his *Confessions*:

> I was furious … Wiring to Figgis to expect me, I caught the next train to London, and strode into his house. There followed a sharp encounter, a battle of words over the art and craft of writing, in which, probably, both were right and both were wrong, for there is no golden rule for writing and, though a man may seem to base his style on this master or that, he must write after his own fashion … You could not move Darrell Figgis; he was doctrinaire and rigid. But something I said must have touched him; he relented, went to his desk, and in my presence, though not at my dictation, wrote a

supplementary and much more acceptable report – one that was to ensure the publication of my book.

It would have been interesting to hear Figgis's version of this episode, because Hine's smug account almost beggars belief. Surely, the Irishman could not have been best pleased by the arrogance of this unknown young author who had burst into his home uninvited. And, if Figgis really did sit down and write a 'much more acceptable report' with Hine looking on, it can only have been because he had realised that this was the only way he was going to get the bloody man out of his house. Hine claims he spent the afternoon listening to Figgis recite poetry and that the two of them parted on good terms. Figgis, alas, was unable to comment on the story when it appeared because, by that time, he was dead.

With this grandiose belief in the quality of his work, Hine determined from the outset that *The History of Hitchin* would be no mere book of reference but a work of art as well. A literary jewel that would be beautiful to look upon, beautiful to hold and beautiful to read. A thousand years of parish life presented in a style that future historians would find hard to better. Thus, and to his credit, he resisted the temptation to regurgitate the writings of those county chroniclers who had gone before him, choosing instead to base his research as far as possible on original documents:

> *The History of Hitchin* (is) a work based not so much on printed matter as on hundreds of thousands of charters, feoffments, Court Rolls, Close Rolls, Patent Rolls, account books minute books, diaries etc that had, first of all, to be discovered and disinterred; and not in one parish or county and country, but in many parishes, counties and countries. That is the special fascination and difficulty of local history; the records of your parish will be scattered over the face of the earth; and even in your own soil you need to dig not one spit deep but two. Small things and tiny parishes, slipping more easily through nooks and crannies of time, sink deeper into oblivion.

When at last the materials are brought up to the light, you must work, as it were, in mosaic; no longer an historical artisan but an historical artist. Building up, if you can, an authentic picture of the past; assembling your innumerable isolated facts of every conceivable colour; fitting, joining, compacting them together into a preordained design.

Because Hine had managed to drum up an encouraging number of advance subscriptions, Allen & Unwin proposed a print run of one thousand copies. Rarely had they met an author with such an overwhelming enthusiasm for his project. Aided by Florence, Hine continued to canvass orders, writing scores of letters to friends and acquaintances throughout Hertfordshire and beyond. So it was that, half way through publication, the list of advance subscribers shot well past the thousand mark and the print run had to be doubled. The company's autocratic chairman, Sir Stanley Unwin, declared it 'a bloody marvel' – apparently the only occasion the Old Man had been heard to swear during the whole of his career. Over at the printing works, however, somewhat stronger oaths were heard from time to time when it dawned on the compositors and binders that the figure of Hine was going to be hovering over them, hawk-like, throughout the project.

Most authors, having given a general idea of how they would like their book to look, are usually content to leave matters of design and layout to the publishers' experts. But Hine had his own plans and insisted upon controlling every step of the operation. The typeface, the ornate drop-letters for the start of each chapter, the expensive paper, the gilt edges, the special inks, the positioning of illustrations and the elaborate blocking of the binding – all were his personal choice and many elements reflected his delight in the look of 17th-century books. The publishers could recall only one other author – the wood-engraver Robert Giddings – who had been as meticulous. Back in Hitchin, Hawkins & Co. saw even less of their elusive clerk as he disappeared on almost daily visits 'to my London publishers.'

Senior compositors working on the page layouts would stand patiently to one side while the author cogitated over just where precisely the Lucas sketch of Quaker women playing chess should be placed. If he was not visiting, he was writing to them. The editorial team found themselves having to cope with his sudden decisions to re-write part of the text after an idea came to him late in the day. Everyone struggled to make sense of the handwriting. Although Philip Unwin looks back upon the labour pains that preceded his first publication with some affection, much may be deduced from his aside that, whenever the words 'Mr Hine of Hitchin' were spoken in the typists' room, they were greeted by 'a barely suppressed groan.' Nevertheless, he admits that 'after Herculean labours on everybody's part, a very fine local history resulted.'

Indeed, when Volume One was published, it attracted widespread and enthusiastic reviews. Most highlighted Hine's ability to enliven dull historical facts with the human touch. 'No mere dry-as-dust collection of documents but a vivid narrative of English country life,' opined the magazine *Public Opinion*. 'A very engaging story as well as a painstaking antiquarian document,' wrote a *Country Life* reviewer. 'The past is vivid; the bones of old account books are clothed in flesh and blood, so they fill the stage as a thrilling drama.' Even in faraway South Africa, his sister Ione opened her copy of *The Cape Times* to find a reviewer enthusing that 'Mr Hine has all the qualities of the antiquarian. The patience, the thoroughness, the passion for the past; but he has also the gifts that so many antiquarians lack. He can make dry bones live.'

Most significantly, *The History of Hitchin* impressed many leading historians of the day, some of whom had given help and advice during Hine's years of research. Professor George Macaulay Trevelyan, the author of *A History of England*, wrote 'I have nothing but admiration for the method, plan and style of it. It illustrates by local facts the general outlines of the military, financial and religious history of the nation as one knew it. That is its great fascination.' So in a sense Hine had confounded Herman Melville's dictum of the need for a mighty theme. By setting his parish's history in a national context, he had shown how the traumatic upheavals in England's history came to affect ordinary men and women, squire and peasant, as they went about their lives

in a typical English market town. As he was fond of inscribing in
the front of the book when asked for his signature:

> Thus in a thousand pages have I sought to show
> He knows not England that does not Hitchin know.

In 1929, the year that Volume Two was published, Hine was
offered Fellowships of both the Society of Antiquaries and the
Royal Historical Society. Recognition that persuaded the fuddy-
duddies of the East Herts Archaeological Society that it was time
to forgive the younger Hine's earlier transgressions concerning
the 'Roman urn' and allow him membership. By this time the
historian was putting the finishing touches to *Hitchin Worthies*,
now widely regarded as the most readable of the trilogy. Produced
to the same high standards, it attracted yet more enthusiastic
reviews, setting the seal on his reputation. The book also added a
feather to the cap of Allen & Unwin, when it was chosen as one
of the fifty best produced books of 1932. A fact of which Hine was
enormously proud and of which he painstakingly reminded the
reader whenever called upon to autograph a copy:

> It should be placed on record that this book was chosen, out of
> 22.000, as one of the fifty best-produced works of the year (1932)
> and with the other 49 was exhibited in most of the European
> capitals and in the U.S.A.

Among Hine's fans on the other side of the Atlantic was a
distinguished American scholar named Walter Muir Whitehill.
A former Director and Librarian of the Boston Athenaeum, it
was Dr Whitehill who described the language of *Hitchin Worthies*
as 'so fine that the book should be read aloud.' In a preface for
Eric Moore's reprint in 1974, he describes how he enjoyed this
experience when his wife read it to him as they drove across
Maine and New Brunswick on their way to a fishing holiday. 'The
eighteenth century highwayman John Everett and Bishop Mark
Hildesley enlivened our passage through hundreds of miles of
evergreen forest,' he wrote. 'I will long associate certain otherwise
unmemorable stretches of road with Captain Robert Hinde of

Preston Castle, the original of Sterne's *Uncle Toby*, and other worthies restored to life by Reginald Hine.

* * *

One unfortunate side effect caused by the stresses involved in completing the Hitchin trilogy was that it brought Hine once more to the brink of a nervous breakdown. Since the end of the Great War his neurasthenia had troubled him less, a blessing he attributed as much to his Quaker friends as anyone else. One of the many physicians he consulted during his dark days had suggested that the therapeutic qualities of a Society of Friends' meeting might provide an antidote to the problems caused by his highly-strung introspection. Having already made friends with a number of the community during his researches, he took to joining them at their meetings. The doctor's theory seemed to work but, as Hine later reported, it took a while:

> Quakers are not easy of approach, and at first I was deterred.
> Myself addicted to the 'distemper of enthusiasm,' as they would
> term it, I was the more repelled by their guarded speech; their icy
> understatement. I used to pretend that the temperature fell thirty
> degrees whenever I came into the presence of Friends. I forgot
> to be grateful for the opportunity thus afforded to reduce my
> own. Always there was the silent reproof of their better practice;
> their sad renunciation of colour; their grey prohibiting outlook
> on the arts and graces of this present life. But in time these small
> vexations vanished before the sheer goodness and constancy of
> Friends: their meekness and moderation: their 'holy care' to live up
> to 'the fine principle of light and love.'

A new and embarrassing side effect of this latest bout of illness was that Hine developed alopecia, which caused his hair to fall out in great tufts. The temporary baldness forced him to wear a skullcap for a while. One day early in 1928 he fell into conversation with a young Hitchin man named Bill Upchurch, whose father ran an antiques gallery in the town and who – although still in his early twenties – had already lost most of his hair. Not realising that the reasons for Bill's baldness were genetic rather than neurological, Hine offered to put him in touch with the specialist who had treated him. His letter, while interesting medically, also demonstrates the lengths he was prepared to go to help people:

Riddy Shott,
Hitchin, Herts.
2.ii.28

Dear Mr Upchurch,

Of course I am delighted to help any fellow sufferer; especially one I respect as much as I do you.

This alopecia is (according to the best opinion) a nervous disease. It is brought on in my case by a partial nervous breakdown due to overwork. And you work even harder that I do. One has to treat the nerves. With rest. With medicine like valerian or digitalis*. With more exercise and more change. You'd probably find it difficult, as I did, to get away – but a change is most remedial.

The best remedy, however, as I am convinced, is the treatment by electricity known as violet ray. I have seen some remarkable cases of alopecia recently (some of them total) at Lavender Croft opposite me where I still go for treatment. Mr Gilbert Hayden there is a very clever man and what is better he is very cheap. I've sent lots of patients there and all of them have blessed me. It not only brings back the hair but it tones up the whole system and gives one about 30% more life – a thing that is important to busy people.

Come and have a talk some time at the office or at my home; and if you care to see Mr Hayden and make your own impression I will introduce you. One feels awful without hair – a sort of inferiority complex sets in. I can fully sympathise and what is more I can help you to its cure.

Yours sincerely,
Reginald L Hine

---

* Herbal medicines. Valerian is used as a sedative and Digitalis to stimulate the heart muscle.

There was another factor contributing to Hine's delicate nervous state at this time. By his own admission, the first three decades of the twentieth century had been the best years of his life but, with the publication of *The History of Hitchin*, he must have realised that his days of privilege at Hawkins & Co. were numbered. According to Basil Donne-Smith, the law firm underwent something of a shake-up in the 1920s. 'They had lost the management of the Priory estates and there had been changes in the partnership, too,' he recalled in his memoir. 'The redistribution of wealth had begun to make life a more serious matter even for the gentry of a country market town like Hitchin.'

One result of these changes was that Hine's mentor Onslow Times, by then in his late seventies, had handed over control of the firm to his long-time partner, Arthur Lindsell, and a nephew Major Wilberforce Times. The old man eventually retired in 1929 following a serious illness but recovered sufficiently to enjoy several more years of activity, playing golf and continuing to immerse himself in the life of the Church and other local causes close to his heart. He also lived long enough to see Hine legalize the fraudulent entry *'Profession – Solicitor'* that his clerk had written on his wedding certificate and in his passport many years earlier. With his book safely published, the historian decided to concentrate for a while on the job 'for which it had *not* pleased God to call him' back in 1901. As he approached his fiftieth birthday Hine sat his final law examinations and was at last admitted as a solicitor on July 1st 1933.

When Onslow Times died a year later at the age of 83, it could have been the death of the monarch so far as the people of Hitchin were concerned. Shops were closed, blinds were drawn and flags flew at half-mast. Throughout the night preceding the funeral his body lay in state in St Mary's Church, with men from the Hitchin Church Adult Class taking turns to keep vigil over the coffin. 'It was difficult to number the vast congregation,' the *Hertfordshire Express* reported later, 'but never in living memory has there been a greater gathering in Hitchin's parish church.' Hine was among the principal mourners that day, occupying a place on the front pew with members of the Times family. His employer, Arthur

Lindsell, sat just behind with the entire staff of Hawkins & Co. Neither Florence Hine nor her daughter were present but the card with the Hine wreath read: *'From Florence, Felicity (your god-daughter) and Reg (your old articled clerk and intimate friend for 34 years) in affectionate remembrance.'*

The service was conducted by the Bishop of St Albans the Right Reverend Michael Furse, supported by fifteen clergy from North Hertfordshire parishes. Afterwards, the many townsfolk who had been unable to get into the church joined the cortege that followed Onslow Times on his final journey through the market town. Walking all the way up Hitchin Hill to the cemetery, where the bishop committed his 'dear old friend' to rest in the family grave. However, it was Hine who had the final word when, on the Monday following the funeral, the *Times* newspaper, appropriately, carried this tribute:

William Onslow Times was one of those men who seem to epitomise the life history of the towns in which they dwell. This last 60 years and more his name and that of Hitchin and the county of Hertford and the diocese of St Albans have been inseparably allied. Not in the least an officious man, he nevertheless held every imaginable office. In parish and church affairs he was the inevitable man. In the days of his youth they were wont to call John Hawkins (father of Lord Brampton) his revered master "The King of Hitchin" and those who came after might justly have styled Mr Times as its president, for he presided over all things. Once or twice I heard him affectionately described as "Ancient and Modern Times" and the phrase does suggest something of his vast experience of public life, and his sanguine, sympathetic outlook upon times present. It was better than poring over tomes of social history to hear him talking of the days when he used to sit as Clerk to the Turnpike Trustees, and complain of rates at 2s 6d and income tax at 2d in the pound.

Elected in 1876 as the youngest County Court Registrar in England he had, upon his retirement in 1929, the control of five Courts with jurisdiction extending over seven counties. Magistrates might come and magistrates might go, councillors, vestrymen, vicars also but Mr Times went on as Clerk and Parish Clerk apparently for ever. Thirty, 40, 50 years seemed nothing to him. On one school alone he served as manager for 63 years. Men marvelled at his easy mastery of the law, his knowledge of the niceties of procedure, his success in that most difficult art, the art of managing men. But all that came out of a lifetime of hard and intelligent study, and a shrewd insight into human character. Truly, the little community that he helped to lead forward from the Victorian into the Edwardian and lastly into the Georgian era moved not with the times but with Times. The name of Onslow Times is now transmitted to a nephew. Of some of his life work the continuity is well assured. There are no children to rise up and call him blessed; but he was father-in-the-law, guide, counsellor and friend to hundreds of families who will cherish his memory and live on in the light of his precepts.

This eulogy to 'The Master' also marked a significant turning point in Hine's life. For at the offices of Hawkins & Co. steps were already being taken to end the easy-going relationship that had long existed between the historian and his employers.

HITCHIN QUAKERESSES AT CHESS
Drawing by Samuel Lucas

[5]
Times of Change

ONE AFTERNOON IN 1932, the partners and staff of Hawkins & Co. assembled in the garden behind their Portmill Lane premises for a group photograph [*Illus*.33]. In the resulting image one individual comes across very clearly as the odd man out. Whereas everyone else has responded to the photographer's request to 'Look this way please,' Reginald Hine has not. Instead, he stands with his hands in his pockets looking away at something in the middle distance. Perhaps he preferred to be photographed in this Victorian profile but if ever there was a symbolic picture of a man who was no longer part of the team, this is it.

Following the demise of his father figure it was probably inevitable that, although it was the last thing he wanted, Hine and Hawkins & Co. would part company. In the lean years of the 1930s, the new senior partners, Arthur Lindsell and Major Wilberforce Times, could no longer afford to carry passengers. The first sign of their disapproval of Hine's tendency to give his hobby priority over his work came in 1933 when he completed his articles and was finally admitted as a solicitor. Despite the fact that he had been with the firm for more than thirty years, he was not invited to become a partner. He was instead promoted from solicitor's clerk to assistant solicitor and retained as a salaried member of staff.

Although there were no outward signs of unpleasantness, the partners' frustration with Hine's attitude left a clear impression upon the younger members of their families. Major Times' daughter, Margaret McNeill, recalled: 'I'm afraid Mr Hine was not very popular in the office. He had a room to himself and instead of working for the firm he spent all his time on his books. Eventually Daddy and his partner Arthur Lindsell told him he would have to leave. After that, things went rather cool between us, although he did still come up to the house from time to time and he gave me one of his books for a wedding present. But he was not my mother's favourite man by any means.' Similar recollections from a member of the Lindsell family were expressed rather more bluntly: 'In the end the partners got pretty sick of Hine. He was being paid by the partnership yet he did damn all for them. He occupied space; he occupied a desk, yet spent all the time working on his books. My understanding is that he was virtually turfed out of the firm in the end.'

It could not have been easy for Arthur Lindsell. Like John Hawkins and Onslow Times before him, he was a dedicated 'Hitchin' man who had the welfare of the town close to his heart. In 1928, he had been instrumental in forging a closer link between the professional and business communities when he organised a meeting at his offices that led to the founding of Hitchin Rotary Club. He was later elected their first President. So having to persuade the town's celebrated historian that it might be better if he moved on to pastures new would have required considerable tact. One can only imagine how it came about. A suggestion, perhaps, that as the firm was unable to offer him a partnership he might feel he could do better were he to set up on his own account when a suitable opportunity arose. No hurry, of course, but something to bear in mind. Whatever the case, Lindsell and Times did not have long to wait because in late 1935 Hine received the offer of a partnership in another law firm.

It came from Reginald Hartley, who at that time ran a practice in the small and rather isolated market town of Royston, in the north east of the county. In 1935 he decided to expand by opening a second office. The reason he chose Hitchin may have been that, as one of the regular prosecuting solicitors for Hertfordshire Police, it made sense to have a base in the town that was then the divisional police headquarters for North Hertfordshire. So when premises became available in Bancroft just across the road from the police station he was quick to secure the tenancy. Quite how the two Reginalds came to join forces is not recorded but Hartley must have reckoned that Hine's high profile in the community could only be good for business. Added to which, the alliterative title *Hartley & Hine* had a rather splendid ring to it. So, in January 1936, public notice was given: 'That Mr Reginald Hartley has now opened an office at Hitchin and taken into partnership Mr Reginald L. Hine with whom he is practising at that office under the style of Hartley & Hine. The practice at Royston is being carried on as previously under the style of Reginald Hartley.' At this stage Hawkins & Co. do not appear to have voiced any objection to the fact that a former member of their staff was involved in setting up a rival practice barely two hundred yards from their own offices in Portmill Lane.

Hartley & Hine occupied the first and second floors of 109 Bancroft, one of the street's attractive older properties that had previously been run as a guesthouse. The new partners were fortunate that the lease they took over still had eight years to run. Once installed, Hine soon set about giving his office a personal touch. He hung the large sash windows with tasteful velvet curtains and adorned the walls with paintings by Samuel Lucas and Canaletto, his favourite Italian artist. He acquired a large leather chair and antique desk and set them throne-like upon a low dais, to give him height and thereby authority over those who sat before him. As time went by, the historian's gift for procuring antiques (of which more later) resulted in the room becoming as cluttered with furniture as those at Willian Bury. 'Come into my museum,' he would joke to his clients. The bookseller Eric Moore likened the experience to stepping onto the set of an Edwardian play. He went one day to look at some antiquarian books that the historian had decided to sell. It was the first time the two men had met:

> Dressed in a wine-coloured velvet jacket, flamboyant bow tie and glistening ornamental fob, Hine was sitting in a richly ornate chair at a similarly decorated desk, raised on a low dais. Around him was his choice collection of antiques – Queen Anne cabinets, Sheraton chairs, two grandfather clocks, silver candlesticks and a 19th century truncheon hanging alongside the Samuel Lucas water-colours … I need not have been over-awed by Hine's museum for he had that rare ability of disarming the most dedicated businessman. Pushing his antique-white telephone and legal papers to one side and opening a large cupboard bulging to bursting point

with books, he soon had the volumes arrayed on his desk.

How reverently he handled those relics of the past and (to use his own words) 'thrilled to the touch old vellum.' Hine had put off the lawyer and become the antiquary. His eyes glinted with excitement as we spent a delightful hour; he discussing the books with such enthusiasm that I had great difficulty in keeping the purpose of my visit in mind. But there was no argument to spoil the atmosphere. When I left I had made a friend and established goodwill; and acquired a nice collection of books into the bargain. These volumes were no mere throw-outs; all bore the hallmark of a rare collector of unusual literary lore and historical anecdotes – a perceptive mind eager to fathom the complexity of human nature.

Hine's tailor Philip Stone had no illusions about the set-up at Hartley & Hine and was not taken in by the historian's sense of theatre:

I would say that Mr Hartley was the solicitor in that partnership; a solicitor in the proper sense of that word. Mr Hine seemed to *play* at being a solicitor. I reckon he would have made a first class actor. Every time I went to see him he always had this huge pile of important looking documents in front of him. I would have to sit there for several minutes while he went through this routine of putting them into neat piles and pushing them around the desk before beginning business. I came to the conclusion that it was all part of the act, just like the white telephone. But he had a kind heart and liked to please. Whenever he knew I was going to call on him he always made sure he was wearing one of the suits I had made.'

* * *

Hine's literary output continued throughout the 1930s, although not all of it was new. It consisted mainly of locally produced booklets containing revamped material that had already appeared in *The History of Hitchin*. There was *A Short History of St Mary's Hitchin* (40 pages), *The History of Hitchin Grammar School* (68 pages), *The Story of Methodism at Hitchin* (16 pages) and *The Story of the Sun Hotel* (24 pages). Then, towards the end of 1934, a weighty and expensively produced tome entitled *The Natural History of the Hitchin Region* made its appearance and promptly sold more than a thousand copies. It was published by Hitchin and District Regional Survey Association, an august body founded in 1929 by a group of natural history enthusiasts. Rather like their opposite numbers in East Herts Archaeological Society, they sought to encourage the local population and young people in particular to take a greater interest in the natural history of their region. At their helm was Mr E.F.D. Bloom, the area's Inspector of Schools; a savant of the old school who was held in some awe by the teaching profession. Mr Bloom was one of seven local naturalists and scientists who each contributed a chapter to the book. Hine acted as editor and wrote an introduction.

Despite the fact that its success was the result of a team effort, so far as the public was concerned it was 'Mr Hine's new book.' In a glowing review the *Hertfordshire Advertiser* reported: 'Mr Hine has caused to be published today (Friday) his fourth and last Hitchin book ... It marks the completion of the historical survey of Hitchin, which he undertook twenty years ago.' Once again, generous offers of sponsorship enabled the Association to produce a locally printed volume of almost the same high quality as *The History of Hitchin* and to sell it for only 7s 6d, about a third of the real cost. The publishers were also able to indulge themselves by ordering a special Natural History map of the region from the Ordnance Survey. This was inserted in a pocket inside the back cover of each volume and cost nearly half the price of the book to produce. There was also a limited luxury edition, extravagantly bound in soft leather, which found its way to a number of favoured subscribers and sponsors. Mr Bloom declared that no better book on local natural history had been produced anywhere in England. He was perhaps being a trifle optimistic when he announced that it would encourage young readers back to 'the simple and lasting joys of life instead of spending their leisure time on the ephemeral and frothy pleasures of the cinema, the wireless and the dance hall.'

In fact, this was not *quite* Hine's last Hitchin book. In 1938, as if to test the local market to its limit, he produced *The Story of Hitchin Town*, another slim volume featuring a collection of contemporary pen and ink sketches and a new Hine essay on the market town. This was the result of collaboration with Gerard Ceunis, a Belgian artist and businessman who came to England with his family as a refugee at the beginning of the First World War. Having chosen to settle in Hitchin, Mr Ceunis opened *Maison Gerard*, a fashion shop for women on the corner of Market Place and Churchyard. Along the Gosmore Road, he built himself a house, complete with artist's studio in the roof. Rather like Hine, he was also a man torn two ways, in his case between the demands of business and the love of painting. Although his style was not universally popular he was admired for his treatment of light in his paintings and sketches.

* * *

The 1930s also saw a major change in the Hine family's domestic life. After twelve years at Riddy Shott Reg and Florence moved from Hitchin to a much larger house a couple of miles outside the town in the village of Willian. The move had been precipitated by Florence's concerns over the health of her mother. By this time, Mrs Pyman was in her seventies and becoming too frail to live alone in her large London town house. As the only daughter, it fell to Florence to persuade her mother to sell up and return to Hertfordshire to live with her. Because Frank Pyman was still detained in the Priory Asylum, his wife was required once again to seek approval from the Dickensian-sounding Master in Lunacy to put the house on the market and look for a property in North Hertfordshire that would be large enough for her family to share.

The opportunity came when the Diocese of St Albans decided that the house occupied by the vicar of All Saints' Church at Willian was too large and expensive to maintain. Standing in more than nine acres of grounds, the Old Rectory had been built in the first half of the 18th century. A wing was added about a hundred years later. From the Pymans' point of view the property was ideal. The numerous bedrooms, the old servants' quarters and a huge kitchen and cellar meant that it could be adapted so that several members of the family could live under the same roof while still enjoying a reasonable amount of privacy and independence.

Thus, on 2nd September 1929, as principal trustees of Frank Pyman's estate, Mrs Pyman and her second son Geoffrey, purchased the Old Rectory from the Church of England for £3,850. It was also agreed that the Pyman estate would provide an annual grant of one thousand pounds for the upkeep of the property. Such was Church Law in those days that the disposal of any of their property required approval from the highest level. Consequently, the Deed of Sale carries the signatures, not only of the incumbent and his bishop, but that of the current Archbishop of Canterbury, Cosmo Gordon, as well. In due course, the new owners renamed the house Willian Bury, a name that continues to the present day. There was only one problem when the move took place. Mrs Pyman had collected so much furniture during the course of her life that several large pantechnicons were required to bring it from London. As a result, most of the rooms had to be packed with far more furniture than they really needed and one bedroom had to be used purely to store pieces for which no other place could be found. It remained like that the whole of the time that the family was there.

Florence cared for her mother at the Bury throughout the last eighteen months of her life and was with her when she died on 11th March 1931, aged 73. Frank Pyman outlived his wife by ten years, his long and tragically unfulfilled life ending at the Priory Asylum on 22nd March 1941. He was 86 and had been there for more than half his life. Frank and his wife are buried in Hitchin Cemetery, sharing a grave with their youngest child, Cyril, who had died in 1900 at the age of eight when the family was living at The Oaks. Frank Pyman left an impressive estate valued at £334,697, to be shared equally between his three surviving children; his sons Frank Junior and Geoffrey and his daughter Florence. Willian Bury was deemed to be a part of Florence's share and was transferred to her on 10th October 1942.

With such a dreamer for a husband it is hardly surprising that Mrs Hine emerged as the dominant personality in her household. Although she continued to share her Reg's love of poetry, music and languages (speaking French and Italian quite fluently) she also had a liking for action and adventure; a preference illustrated by her life-long interest in the Girl Guide movement. Shortly after her fiftieth birthday, she killed a crocodile with a single rifle shot when it was threatening members of her family as they bathed in the River Nile. Having learned to drive in 1908, she developed a love for fast open-top cars and, unusually for a woman in that era, thought nothing of motoring across Europe without the protection of a male companion [*Illus.* 30].

Having completed her own education at a finishing school, Florence decided that their daughter should do the same. So at the age of sixteen Felicity was transferred from Hitchin Girls' Grammar School to The Downs, a private college at Seaford in West Sussex. By this time she had grown into an attractive young woman, taking after her father more than her mother both in physique and temperament. In 1934, she obtained a place at St. Hilda's College, Oxford, where she read history. Felicity was later to tell her children: 'I had such a good time there that it's a wonder I passed any exams.' Suspecting that her daughter may have been having *too* good a time, Mrs Hine took to driving to Oxford every weekend, ostensibly on 'friendly visits,' but really to check up on Felicity's social life and friends.

Back in Hertfordshire for the summer holidays Felicity joined a group of amateur Shakespearean players and took leading roles in several open-air productions. Twice, she was cast opposite a little-known amateur performer who would one day receive a knighthood for his work as one of the most popular character actors of the late 20th century. At that time Sir Michael Hordern was a young commercial traveller working for the Educational Supply Association at Stevenage, selling desks, blackboards and exercise books to schools in East Anglia. Before becoming a professional actor in 1937, he belonged to several amateur drama groups in the district. In *As You Like It*, presented in the grounds of Hitchin Priory in 1935, he and Felicity were cast as Orlando and

Rosalind. The following year they played opposite each other in *Loves Labour's Lost*. Sir Michael (1911-1995) makes brief mention of these 'out-of-door' productions in his autobiography *A World Elsewhere*. He also confesses that he had a number of affairs with his leading ladies over the years. Only he and Felicity would know if these began as early as 1935 but the young Hordern was certainly a regular caller at Willian Bury while the shows were in progress. A compulsive tree-climber since early childhood he left the Hines a memento of one visit by climbing the tallest elm tree in the garden and taking a bird's-eye photograph of the house and grounds [*Illus.* 35].

Whether or not the pair enjoyed a brief summer romance would have depended upon Felicity's love life at Oxford at that time. Despite her mother's vigilance it was there that she met the man she would eventually marry. Bill McEwen, a student from Port Elizabeth University in South Africa, had won a Rhodes Scholarship to Oxford and was reading Economics at University College. Apparently he first noticed Felicity because of a trait inherited from her father. As he put it later: 'She was the best looking girl at Oxford at that time, with legs that went on for ever.' Unfortunately for the couple, Felicity's choice of husband did not go down well with her mother. In common with most middle-class *maters* of that period Florence had firm ideas about the kind of man she wanted her daughter to marry and Bill McEwen, with his 'colonial' birth and strong South African accent, did not qualify for consideration. Such were the snobbish social taboos of those days. Sir Michael Hordern, incidentally, recalled how his father, a career naval officer, stopped him and his sister from playing with two very nice children who they befriended in their Devon village because they were not considered to be 'our type.' Their father was a vet, you see.

Bill McEwen's family had emigrated to South Africa from Northern Ireland in 1860. His father was a railway surveyor who rose to become general manager of Nigerian Railways and was eventually appointed an acting governor of that country. Bill was a popular student at Oxford and a member of the University Air Squadron where he won his pilot's wings. It is not hard to imagine how this dashing figure became as attractive to Felicity she was to him. Like so many loving and obedient daughters throughout history, her eyes were opened by the hitherto unknown freedoms of university life and she made the most of them. In the end this rather gentle girl found herself caught between two much stronger characters, but such was the strength of her love for Bill that – probably for the first time in her life – she defied her mother. Her sons believe Felicity's acceptance of their father's proposal was probably as much an act of rebellion as it was an act of love.

Bill and Felicity (both only children) were married at All Saints' Church, Willian, on 1st June 1938. The Hon. John McEwen and his wife made the long journey from their home in Lagos to see their son married and practically the whole village turned out to see his bride walk the short distance from her home to the church on her father's arm [*Illus.* 37 & 38]. Following the service more than one hundred guests attended the reception in a marquee in the Bury grounds. A few days later, Florence hosted a coffee morning for her fellow members of Willian Women's Institute so that they could inspect the display of gifts the couple had received.

Fortunately, the risky combination of courtship and study did not do too much damage to the real objective of Bill and Felicity's years at Oxford. Both obtained degrees with 2nd class honours and, although Bill was disappointed not to get a first, his B.A. was sufficient to secure him a post in the old Colonial Office. Once there, he immediately found himself attached to the Sudan Political Service, through which Britain was then administering Africa's largest country in a joint operation (on paper, at least) with Egypt. Given his background in economics, Bill was assigned to the Finance Department, which oversaw Sudan's budget and economy. Following a short honeymoon he duly sailed for Khartoum, leaving his bride at home in Hertfordshire.

Florence Hine tried hard not to let her disapproval of her son-in-law upset family relationships. The three went on a number of holidays together and, early in 1939, when Bill was due home on leave, she drove Felicity all the way to Genoa, to meet the ferry that brought him over from North Africa.

At this time, of course, much of Italy was in the grip of

Mussolini's Fascist gangs. Curious to discover why *il Duce* was arousing such fervour among some Italians and fear among others, Florence decided to go to one of the rallies and was pleased to discover that her Italian was good enough to understand the gist of Mussolini's ranting. To the end of her days, though, Florence's disdain for her son-in-law's colonial background never wavered, this despite the fact that he worked hard to lose his South African accent. Indeed, by the time his children were born, it had all but disappeared. Far from being overwhelmed by his redoubtable mother-in-law Bill frequently resorted to humour as a way of rebutting some of her more irritating pronouncements. A point illustrated by the opening words of an otherwise friendly letter, written to Florence while he was serving with the Royal Air Force during the war. It began: *'My dear Hitler. . .'*

Having qualified as a pilot at Oxford, Bill McEwen left Sudan for neighbouring Egypt to enlist in the R.A.F. as soon as war broke out. From there he flew on several bombing missions over Greece before being posted back to England. The timing of that posting almost certainly saved his life. The day after he left for home, most of his colleagues were killed when enemy aircraft ambushed their flight as it was on its way to a raid. During the remainder of the war McEwen completed three tours of duty with different squadrons. He had a spell as a test pilot; he flew unarmed Mosquitoes on reconnaissance missions over Scandinavia and later joined Coastal Command where he was awarded a D.F.C. and bar after taking part in hazardous low-level bombing attacks on U-boats.

Felicity moved home thirteen times as she followed her husband from one posting to another. The couple's three sons, Andrew, Michael and William, were all conceived during the war years. Each time, Felicity returned to Willian Bury to be able to give birth to her children 'at home.' We get a brief flash of Hine's pride in his son-in-law's exploits (and on becoming a grandfather) in one of his wartime letters to fellow historian James Curry: 'We are all cheery and well at home. My daughter and her son are living with us whilst her gallant husband is in Iceland. He won the D.F.C. last month and there was much in the London papers over his exploits in destroying a submarine. His son (all of seventeen months) is so proud that he won't speak to anyone under the rank of Group Captain!'

Throughout the war years, Hine the lawyer found himself having to work harder than ever before. To a client whose house sale he was handling he wrote wistfully: 'I am now much more, I add almost alas, the solicitor than ever, and work three times as hard as I used to with Hawkins & Co.' One side of his work that he particularly enjoyed was drawing up wills. He regarded will making as 'the most pleasing and human part of a lawyer's practice.' In his *Confessions*, he states that, if he were purchasing a law firm, one of his first questions would be: 'How many wills do you have in safe custody, and in how many of these have the partners been appointed executors?' He goes on:

> In my time I must have drawn up a couple of thousand wills, but naturally the pace quickens in times of pestilence or peril. When I wrote *The History of Hitchin* I was interested to see how clients flocked into the office of Ralph Skynner (one of the founding partners of Hawkins & Co.) at the time of the Great Plague of 1665, to make their wills . . . I well remember the will-making rush of 1940 when the 'pestilence that walketh in the darkness and the destruction that wasteth at noonday' were decimating England. A bomb that fell one night on a nearby village brought me three terrified testatorial civilian clients the next morning. Not knowing what another night might bring, they all demanded to sign there and then.

In between will making and conveyancing Hine was occasionally called on to put his pen to use to boost public morale. In April 1941 as 'our foremost man of letters' he was invited to write a short piece for the newspapers, urging support for the nation's War Weapons Week:

> At the time of the Battle of Hastings the tenants of the Royal Manor of Hitchin paid 106 pounds weight of silver into the war chest of Harold their lord and king. Before the Battles of

Agincourt, Crecy and Poitiers the men of Hitchin fetched down their weapons from the walls of St Mary's and marched away to strike a blow for England. Now, in this critical hour, in this Battle for Britain, and for the cause of human freedom everywhere, gallant men of the same township are defending the right on land and sea and in the air. We who stay at home can at least strengthen their hands for war, and furnish them with weapons by offering our money – money that is more than ever 'the very sinews of war.'

Given his personal health problems, Hine seems to have thrived well throughout the war years. Despite the economic restraints facing the publishing world he settled down to write *Confessions of an Un-Common Attorney*. Unlike the histories, which took twenty years to research and write, this was rattled off in just eighteen months. Shortly after delivering the manuscript to J. M. Dent & Sons in January 1944, he wrote to James Curry: 'It is a big weight off my mind … As the record of a double life in law and literature it has come out, I immodestly think, well.' The public and the literary world thought so too. Dent, sensing they were on to a winner, pulled out the all stops and, despite wartime restrictions on the use of good quality paper and inks, produced a stylish volume to match those of his historical trilogy and to do full justice to the elegance of the author's text.

As has surely become apparent from the extracts already drawn upon, *Confessions* is a frank and witty memoir of Hine's life, told with an infectious enthusiasm that soon has the reader bowling along with him. 'A veritable Joe Miller Jest Book of good stories,' Basil Donne-Smith called it. 'Stories told with the kind of artistry that usually only succeeds with the spoken word. This book has an intensely personal magic. One hears rather than reads, and hears also the author's own delight in the telling. There is a zest and a joy in the writing that captivates and endears; a book with a most rich savour.' It was these qualities that led to it becoming a best seller throughout the English-speaking world. The colourful passages recalling Hine's Edwardian years as an articled clerk have ensured that the book is, to this day, recommended reading for students of Law:

In my work as a budding conveyancer I was placed under the order and disposition of the managing solicitor, William Hammond Hanscombe, who slashed my drafts about, as I considered, just for the sake of slashing, or to keep a mere articled clerk in suitable subjection. But I said nothing because he sprang from a twelfth-century family that was already laying down the law when my people as hinds, or horny-handed tillers of the soil, were still tied hand and foot (*glebae adscripti*) to the lords of their manors. Also, he was a fine figure of a man, especially in the morning, when he appeared in the office in a silk hat and a morning coat. In the afternoon, such was his custom, he walked in wearing a short black coat and a bowler. After tea he strolled in with a lounge suit and cap. When I discussed these descending degrees of dignity with my master-in-the-law, Mr Times, he replied that Hanscombe was right; the gentry always made appointments in the morning; clients grew less distinguished as the day wore on.

Being already on this theme he proceeded to call attention to my own reprehensible habit of cycling in the nine miles from Newnham Hall with no headgear at all. In his view that was not seemly, for, however little I might feel was due to the firm, I should bear in mind that Hitchin was a royal manor, and furthermore that it was locally governed by an Urban District Council of which, and of the earlier Local Board, he had had the honour to be the clerk for close on fifty years. He would not greatly mind what I did and what I wore in the rural district, where the clerk of the council was a rival solicitor, but for the future would I please put on a cap the moment I crossed the boundary?

The sales figures for *Confessions* may seem modest by today's standards but for a publication in the war years, they were very good. In April 1945 the historian was able to write to James Curry: 'My book sold out (5000) in five days. I've had 40 excellent reviews and 700 letters, which I am vainly endeavouring to answer. Yesterday I heard from (a) Colombo (b) Sydney, Australia (c) Brussels, so evidently my publishers have done their best, even in war-time, to spread my book abroad.' Hine frequently reminded friends and audiences that he made no money whatsoever from

any of his books. Reading the next part of this letter one begins
to understand why: 'The second edition should be out at the end
of June. Ask your many friends not to buy, but to put it down on
their *library* lists, for I feel (immodestly, perhaps) that there is
good in the book and I want it to go on doing good.'

The book ran to three editions, but Hine's strange lack of
concern about sales figures became a source of some irritation
for Dent's sales manager, W.H. Thompson. In the run-up to the
launch Hine had become concerned that Hitchin's main retailer,
Burgess Books, was not being allocated sufficient copies. 'I know
you are being good enough to let them have their original order
of 200,' he wrote to Thompson, 'but they now want more. It does
not only concern their shop but also concerns me, because the
majority of my Hitchin friends are planting their orders there,
and as I write my books for the most part for my friends, I do not
want them to be disappointed.'

Thompson's reply put the author politely but firmly in his
place:

'I contend the best service I can offer an Author is to ensure an
even distribution of his book . . . This attitude has the general
support of the booksellers and it is accepted as a fair principle for
everyone. The more copies that go to one particular area, or one
particular bookseller, must re-act to the detriment of other areas,
which in turn annoys the public and booksellers, who end up
by cursing the Author and his Publisher. Generally speaking an
Author's success is assured only when his works are in demand,
not only throughout the country but abroad as well, and until this
object is achieved his success is not assured. I hope you see my
point.'

For several weeks Hine was dashing about the country on
book-signing sessions. *Confessions* was on sale in all the main
London outlets, including Selfridges and Harrods. The author's
insistence upon signing every copy that he came across led Basil
Donne-Smith to observe dryly that, for antiquarians of the future,

the real rarity was going to be the *un*signed copy. Among other 'signing stories' came one from a Hitchin Worthy of the 20th Century, Alderman Beryl Wearmouth M.B.E. (1919-2004).

In 1945, long before her career in local government, Beryl worked as a nurse for Hine's dentist Bill Boyd. One morning, shortly after *Confessions* had been published, Mr Boyd handed her 15s od and sent her off to Burgess Books to pick up his ordered copy. The shop was then at 108 Bancroft, next door to the offices of Hartley & Hine and, as she emerged with the book, who should she bump into but its author. Spotting the purchase Reggie beamed with pleasure. 'Now, Beryl, you *must* come upstairs to my office straight away,' he ordered. 'I have something special for you.' Somewhat overwhelmed by the effusive attention, Beryl allowed herself to be propelled up the staircase into his office, where he took the book from her and proceeded to autograph it. When the book was returned to her, Beryl was horrified to discover that he had written above the signature: *'Specially inscribed for my friend Beryl Wearmouth.'* Not wanting to spoil the author's moment by telling him that it wasn't her book, Beryl thanked him and scuttled back to the surgery wondering how on earth she was going to explain all this to her employer. Roaring with laughter Boyd told his nurse that he now had no option but to give her a Christmas present eight months early. Then he dipped into his pocket and sent her out once more, to buy a second (and potentially rare) unsigned copy for him.

As the acknowledgements pages of his books show, Hine always made sure that any expert who helped him was given the opportunity to check the final page proofs for errors. In July 1944, when the proofs of *Confessions* arrived, he took the precaution of writing to the Secretary-General of the Law Society, T. C. Lund, no less, asking him to arrange for 'some solicitor of standing' to check the pages covering his law career for possible errors. Mr Lund (later Sir Thomas Lund) undertook the task himself and also passed the proofs to the Society's librarian for a second opinion. 'I shall be grateful for any suggestions you have to make for the improvement of my work,' Hine wrote. 'I hate mistakes in books that are meant to last.' Unfortunately there *was* a mistake,

which neither the author nor his eminent legal advisers spotted;
a mistake that proved rather costly and lost him a famous woman
client of whom, up to that point, he had been very fond.

RIDDY SHOTT
showing the extension and gate added by Hine

[6]
Upsetting Ursula

AMONG THE MANY FRIENDS who received a complimentary copy of *Confessions* was one of the best known romantic novelists of the 20th century, Ursula Bloom. Miss Bloom had been a client of Hartley & Hine since she and the historian met by chance in the early 1940s. In his book the lawyer recalls with some affection how she would send him instructions 'in witty, well-turned couplets' and he would do his best to reply in similar fashion. Once, she had presented him with a copy of her latest novel inscribed: *'To the Law, with love, from the Lawless, U.B.'*

However, when 'the Law' made a reciprocal gesture by presenting Miss Bloom with a copy of his *Confessions*, the gift evoked no couplets of thanks. Instead, there arrived an angry letter that began with the chilling question: *'Since when has friendship been an excuse for libel?'* This was followed a few days later by a formal letter from Messrs. Hewett & Pim, solicitors of Reading, informing Hine that they had been instructed by Miss Bloom to take action over an alleged libel contained in the book. Owners of a first edition of *Confessions* will find the offending phrase on page 85. It consists of the seven words that appear in parenthesis towards the end of the following paragraph:

> I have one client - the novelist Ursula Bloom – who on the
> conclusion of a matter sends me an appreciation, or valediction,
> in verse. But then, she is a law unto herself, for, often, the original
> instructions will come tripping along in witty, well-turned couplets,
> and she waits for a witty reply. In the wear and tear of office life,
> and at the uninspired hour of nine in the morning, it can be rather
> trying. But, with the assistance of nimble-minded clerks, and with
> The Rhymers' Lexicon by Loring at my elbow, I will do my best;
> and, when the bill goes in, the gracious lady (if ever she looks at a
> bill) will find this special item: 'To mental strain in replying to your
> letters in verse.'

Miss Bloom claimed that the phrase implied that she never settled her debts. I have to say that on first reading I took it to mean the exact opposite; that here was a person so successful, so wealthy, that she had no need to check the details of each day-to-day bill as it came in. She just paid it. Hine claimed that was what he had intended it to mean. True, he could have made the meaning clearer by writing, for example, 'if ever she *needs to* look at a bill'. But the fact remained that the novelist considered she had been defamed – and her allegation sent a fair ripple of shock waves through the offices of author and publishers alike.

In 1945 Ursula Bloom was in her early 50s and enjoying success as one of the most popular romantic novelists of the post-war era. In a prolific career rivalling that of Dame Barbara Cartland, she produced more than 500 novels, an achievement that was later to earn her a place in *The Guinness Book of Records*. So her legal action was taken very seriously indeed. Hine's publishers placed the matter in the hands of their insurers. The insurers' solicitors decided to instruct Captain Peter Carter-Ruck (1914-2003) a young, up-and-coming solicitor who was destined to become one of Britain's top libel lawyers and earn himself a fearsome reputation among Fleet Street's editors. If the case had come to court he would have been responsible for briefing counsel for the defence.

Fortunately, things didn't get that far. Instead, after numerous written exchanges between four different law firms, the novelist accepted Hine's offer to delete the offending phrase from subsequent reprints and to make a grovelling public apology in the 'Personal' column of *The Times*. This duly appeared in the middle of the front page on Tuesday, 17th April 1945:

MR REGINALD HINE, author of "Confessions of an Un-Common Attorney" (Dent 1945) wishes to make it perfectly clear that the words referring to Miss Ursula Bloom, on page 85 of the book were not intended to suggest or to convey the impression that she did not pay her bills, and Mr Hine greatly regrets any pain and inconvenience these words may have caused Miss Bloom.

At 7s 6d per line, the insertion cost the author just £3.00. However, he also had to pay Ursula's legal costs, which amounted to £31.10s od, and those incurred by his publishers and their insurers, making a total legal bill of £150, which is somewhere in the region of £2,850 based on today's average earnings. One cannot help but feel that all of this was a bit hard on the historian. Ursula Bloom's son, Philip Denham-Cookes could not recall the exact details of 'the argument,' as he called it: 'Only that I do remember my step-father telling my mother he thought she was over-stepping the mark by her reaction. She was not exactly the peaceful individual everyone imagined. She was notoriously careful with her money and rarely paid a bill until the last minute. She also had a number of penny-pinching habits, such as saving Christmas presents that she didn't particularly like in order to give them to someone else the following year.'

Mr Denham-Cookes remembered meeting Hine once, just before *Confessions* was published: 'My mother was staying at Letchworth Hall Hotel. One evening she held a dinner party for my wife and myself and Reginald Hine was a guest. I remember him as a tall, rather gaunt man. He spent the evening talking about dreams, which he claimed he had in colour. He said we should always write our dreams down the following morning because they meant something. My mother thought he was a strange cove.'

* * *

There is an entertaining second act to this legal drama, which almost certainly discloses the real reason why Ursula Bloom reacted in the way she did. Also in *Confessions*, under the heading 'A Clerk in Unholy Orders' (p.28) Hine recalls an incident from his younger days, just before the Great War, when he was in the early stages of researching *The History of Hitchin*. He tells how he spent a weekend with 'a palaeographical parson' – an archivist – who helped him to translate some rare medieval charters relating to Hitchin. Having seen no sign of a wife or housekeeper during his overnight stay at the rectory, he deduced that his host was 'a successful bachelor.' This theory proved to be short-lived. The following morning while out for a short walk before breakfast he bumped into a local farmer who, having learned where he was staying, proceeded to disclose some rather startling information:

> Slowly it came out that not only was the rector married, but his wife and daughter had had to leave him, and there were rumoured to be four or five unofficial wives kept in widely separated places. Possibly that accounted for the fact that the congregation at matins was limited to the gardener and myself. But who was I – a clerk in unholy orders – to sit in judgement on a clerk in holy orders? Whatever his twentieth-century misdeeds, we spent an innocent, studious Sunday afternoon over thirteenth-century deeds, and I went back to my own parish knowing much more of its history than when I left. Thirty years later I offered a lift on the road to a most attractive woman ... Suddenly, from a chance word that fell from her lips, I discovered that she was the daughter of my old palaeographical parson. It was a joyous meeting. At once we were old friends and soon she was one of my clients...'

This 'most attractive woman' was, of course, Ursula Bloom, but because her father was still alive at the time Hine – for obvious reasons – decided not to name either him or his daughter. He also took care to keep the story well away from the chapter in which Ursula is named. However, as the novelist later wrote a book about her father's extra-marital escapades, the full story may now be told.

The Reverend James Harvey Bloom M.A., was a distinguished archivist and researcher whose work – particularly on the records of some of our great churches – led to his being awarded an Honorary Fellowship of the Society of Genealogists. Born at Castle Acre in Norfolk in 1860 he was, for some time, curate at St Andrews, Hertford, where he met and married his long-suffering wife, the former Miss Polly Gardner. In the 1890s, Bloom was appointed Rector of Whitchurch, a poor parish in Warwickshire some three miles south east of Stratford-upon-Avon.

Apart from the church, little now remains of the community

where the Bloom family lived for more than 20 years, and where Ursula grew up. Her father was, by all accounts, a marvellous rector, popular with young and old, rich and poor. A champion of the poor, he would think nothing of spending the night in some agricultural hovel helping a distressed family to nurse their sick child through its crisis. At the other end of the scale, his sharp wit and lively conversation led to numerous invitations to dinner parties in the big houses of the county – occasions to which he and Polly would travel on their bicycles.

It could be said that Harvey Bloom's bicycle was the cause of his downfall. He had never been able to resist an interesting woman and, as he pedalled around the counties of Middle England on his research projects, visiting cathedrals, churches and colleges, he turned the head of many a hopeful spinster. The more serious of Harvey's indiscretions are detailed in his biography *Parson Extraordinary*, which Ursula Bloom published in 1963, nearly 20 years after her father's death. In this she records what proved to be the final straw when, in 1910, Harvey tried to establish a *ménage`a trois* in the rectory. He suggested that, if his latest lady-friend came to stay with them as a guest on a long-term basis, 'the tattlers would be disarmed and no scandal would begin.' That was when his wife walked out on him, taking their daughter Ursula with her.

The Palaeographical Parson (or 'Randy Rector' as he would probably have been dubbed by today's tabloids) eventually left Whitchurch and, indeed, the Church itself and moved to London with the new woman in his life. There, he went into business as plain *J Harvey Bloom, M.A. – Archivist and Genealogist*. It wasn't until many years later that Ursula made contact with her father again, by which time she was married and a successful writer. In the early 1940s, having met Hine in the meantime, she sought the lawyer's help in an attempt to get the wayward Harvey re-established within the Church of England. Recalling his efforts on her behalf, Hine expresses his admiration of the courage she had shown in overcoming the years of poverty that followed her parents' separation:

On her own account, and in spite of terrible handicaps, she has done astonishingly well in the world. But her father had, long since, been unfrocked by the all-knowing bishop, and I was to consider whether I could invoke the cumbrous procedure of the Clerical Disabilities Act, 1873, and get the aged sinner back into the bosom of the Church. Perhaps in appealing to the Archbishop of Canterbury I overstated my case. Was I not writing on behalf of a fine scholar and a friend? But the Primate's reply was chilling. My client's record, black-listed at Lambeth, had made 'distressing reading.' It was 'impossible to re-instate him in the exercise of his ministry.'

Hine's phrase 'unfrocked by the all-knowing bishop' upset Ursula probably more than his comments about her bill paying. As her original letter of complaint goes on to show, the subject may have remained anonymous to every other reader – but certainly not to her:

I don't want to be 'a cantankerous client' but oh dear! My father was never unfrocked. He 'chucked in his hand' I know you cannot libel the dead, but this is quite untrue and I am deeply hurt. The remark (If ever she looks at a bill) has already come home to me and it does infer quite a lot and is vilely untrue. Now you must give me your word that both these remarks come out of any reprint, because I am truly most unhappy that they should have been made, and I am so perturbed that I would like the matter put right…Do please realise that I mean what I say and let me have an immediate reply.

Even after reading the letters exchanged between the different legal camps during this action, one can still only surmise why Ursula was so upset by what Hine had written. It might be because he had upstaged her. His book was published while she was working on her own autobiography, *No Lady meets No Gentleman* (1947) and was already planning her father's biography. Clearly, Hine had not consulted her beforehand and the first she knew of her inclusion was when an eloquently autographed copy arrived at her home out of the blue. There was also the unfortunate coincidence that Hine's rather flippant account of Harvey Bloom's indiscretions was published only a few months after his death in May 1944; a time when all the unhappy memories of Ursula's childhood would have been revived.

Neither would she have liked Hine's final 'wicked thought' in his account of the affair. He recalls that, as he read the letter in which the Archbishop turned down his request for the suspended rector to be re-instated, the idea for 'a scandalous rejoinder' had entered his head. Although he never sent it, he would have *liked* to reply to the Archbishop: 'Your Grace, we grieve to learn that you should despair of our client's spiritual condition, and that you should entertain little or no hope of a genuine repentance. All that we can say to convince you is that, whereas in our client's prime he kept five concubines, now at the age of eighty he has reduced the number to two. Is there not here a reasonable ground for hope?'

Hartley & Hine's original file on this case contains copies of almost one hundred letters that were exchanged during the three months between February and April 1945. The contents of most now seem shamefully trivial in light of the terrible events that were unfolding across Europe at that time. As the horrors of Belsen and Buchenwald were being revealed in the daily press, here were four sets of lawyers solemnly debating the precise wording of a proposed *errata* slip and of Mr Hine's forthcoming apology in *The Times*. There was even a discussion about whether the book should be withdrawn from all libraries until a correction slip had been pasted in every copy. While this was going on, Ursula, somewhat unethically, continued to fire off the occasional taunting letter to Hine at his home address. Her style and punctuation suggest a sherry decanter was close at hand at the time they were written:

Dear Reg,
Honestly, I mean well, only a libel is a libel, it isn't what you
meant – I know you meant nothing but niceness though it was
very naughty about my father, because in Robbie's (her husband's)
presence when driving to Hitchin I had told you the correct facts
– I am afraid when one does this, smarming down doesn't work.

The only thing to do was to harm the book as little as possible, and this is my whole-hearted desire.
God bless the snowdrops and you,
Ursula.

Another day, a postcard arrived at Willian Bury. The address and postage stamp were upside down and on the other side was one of Ursula's more puzzling 'well-turned couplets':

Oh sir you libel me for
Having paid my bills and always by
Return of post; just pause a bit
Before I send you such a writ.
And sir, the answer to this verse
Is coff for me. For t'other, hearse.
From Urse
Who'll take good care she gets the coffee.

In the end, Dent were obliged to print 2,000 correction slips for inclusion in all unsold first edition copies, including those purchased by Boots Chemists and W. H. Smith for their private lending libraries. In recent years, the slip itself has become something of a collector's item and has occasionally been quoted in the correspondence columns of newspapers and literary magazines when readers are discussing their favourite pieces of errata. It reads:

ERRATA
Page 29. *Delete* 'unfrocked by the all-knowing Bishop'
and substitute 'suspended, at his own request.'
Page 85. *Delete* 'if ever she looks at a bill'

As a parting shot, the troublesome Ursula even went out of her way to spoil Reg's big day when he and his book were fêted at a Foyle's Literary Lunch in London. It cannot be mere coincidence that she bought a ticket for the event and then took the trouble to ensure that the two of them met. There is a brief but bitter reference to the incident in a letter to James Curry:

'Am just recovering from an ordeal for, last Friday, Foyles made me their guest of honour at a Literary Luncheon with Compton Mackenzie in the chair and I am not a fluent speaker as you are. However, all went well – in spite of the fact that a lady (Ursula Bloom who has been spitefully at me for libel) had the impudence to be there!'

However, in a letter to one of the law firms that had been involved in the tussle the unlucky historian seems to have recovered some of his sense of humour:

'Mr Hine nearly had a skirmish with Miss Bloom at the Dorchester Hotel Foyle's Literary Luncheon but did not get to grips. Both parties behaved with somewhat strained politeness.'

[7]

Appropriations ... and Apparitions

SHORTLY AFTER THE PUBLICATION of *Confessions of an Un-Common Attorney* in 1945, its author found himself drawn briefly into the controversy surrounding the decision to build Britain's first post-war new town at Stevenage. Asked to represent a farmer whose land was threatened by the development he was present at a public inquiry held at the Cromwell Hotel in Stevenage. It was a crowded affair, involving senior public officials and several legal big guns from London. Geoffrey Mayes was also there, covering the event for the *Hertfordshire Express*, and we are indebted to him for the following gem of gossip. In order to help the inquiry inspector deal with any issues related to land ownership and boundaries, a number of old and very rare maps had been brought over from the county archive at Hertford. At the end of the inquiry, as officials were clearing the tables, one called out in some alarm that a map was missing. Mr Hine, who was just leaving the room, stopped in his tracks. 'Well bless me!' he exclaimed. 'I seem to have it here, under my arm.'

From the day when he first cast a covetous eye on a neighbour's copy of *The Historical Antiquities of Hertfordshire*, the lawyer's eagerness to get his hands on historical documents and artifacts developed into something approaching an obsession. His skill at persuading people to part with personal treasures for the benefit of the community became legendary. There is no more impressive example than that in the section of *Confessions* headed 'Literary Blackmail.' Here he describes with some relish a seven-year campaign conducted against a parsimonious London art collector. The man owned 750 original drawings by the outstanding architectural artist J.C. Buckler (1793-1894) including many depicting churches and other important buildings in Hertfordshire. However, Hine's request for permission to reproduce half-a-dozen in *The History of Hitchin* was met by a blunt refusal. In a story reminiscent of the time he cajoled Dent's reader Darrell Figgis into writing a more favourable report on the manuscript of his first book, the historian admits resorting to a 'dirty tricks' campaign:

> Then I lost my temper, and by registered post dispatched an ultimatum: 'I am engaged as you perhaps do not know, on a work of some historical importance; and it is vital for my purpose to make use of the drawings now lying idle in your hands. In a few months I shall be printing my first volume and shall insert this sentence in italics at the conclusion of my bibliography:
> '*1832. Eleven drawings of Hitchin Church, the Priory, the Grammar School, Skynner's Almshouses, and certain ancient houses in the possession of . . . . . (naming him). Permission to reproduce these has been refused. It is the only incivility the author has experienced in the course of fifteen years' research.*'

The upshot was that the victim then made the fatal mistake of inviting his blackmailer to tea in order that he might put his case in more detail. From that moment on Mr X was fighting a losing battle. Because the collection contains many fine drawings of churches, Hine artfully briefed the Archdeacon of St Albans, Kenneth Gibbs, urging him to write a letter backing up his argument. As a result of their joint campaign the collector was persuaded to donate the entire folio to the diocese for safe keeping in St Alban's Abbey. The drawings were later bound into four handsome leather volumes, each stamped with the county arms and transferred to the County Record Office at Hertford where they remain a popular source of research to this day.

In 1938, many people in the Hitchin area found themselves under a similar pressure to that experienced by Mr X when Hine was co-opted onto the council to help establish the town's first public library and museum. The original building was once a private house named Charnwood, and had been given to the community by Hubert and Wallace Moss of the local grocery family. In company with the schools inspector E. F. D. Bloom and Dr A. H. Foster, an entomologist, Hine set about acquiring exhibits for the museum, nearly all of which had to be begged from local inhabitants. Robert Ashby, the first librarian and museum curator, later wrote: 'A very large proportion of the museum's exhibits came either from Mr. Hine or through his intermediacy. His tall unmistakable figure striding past the library windows – picture or portfolio under arm – regularly betokened something new and interesting for the town's collections. To select one instance among many, it was due to him that the water-colours and sketch-books of Samuel Lucas, works of unparalleled interest and beauty, were presented by the late Stephen Lucas and now form one of the town's most valuable possessions.'

Another of those subjected to Hine's beguiling powers of persuasion was the Reverend Bill Upchurch, who was then helping to run his father's antiques gallery in Bancroft. He remembered Hine as 'a tremendously popular man, with a very engaging personality and wonderfully whimsical sense of humour.' The story Bill had to tell concerns an aeolian harp, a simple sound box that makes attractive harmonies when the wind blows through its strings. It was a very popular feature of Georgian and Victorian households, where it was the custom to place the instrument on the drawing room window ledge to catch the breeze on a summer's evening.

The instrument that belonged to Bill's father had been made in the early 19th century by the Suffolk-born poet Robert Bloomfield, (1766-1823). Bloomfield, who is probably best remembered for his best-selling *The Farmer's Boy*, spent his last years at Shefford, in Bedfordshire, where he made aeolian harps to supplement his meagre income as a shoemaker. Recounting how the harp was passed down through various local families Hine concluded: 'It is now in the possession of William Septimus Upchurch of Hitchin.' Not for long though, as his son ruefully explained:

My father had bought the harp among some odds and ends during a house clearance sale. Hine spotted it in our shop window one day and came in to examine it. When he found Bloomfield's signature upon it he became very excited and started to use all his persuasive powers to get me to donate it to the new museum. Eventually I agreed and handed it over to him. I think it would be fair to say he more or less appropriated it.

Bill left Hitchin in 1935 and, following an eventful life as a Baptist minister and missionary in the Far East, he returned to the town in the 1970s to retire. However, when he called at the museum one day to see if his harp was still on display he was disappointed. Although early records confirmed that Hine had delivered it there some forty years earlier, the harp itself could not be found. 'Naturally, I was very upset,' Mr Upchurch said. 'It was suggested to me that Hine may have borrowed it for one of his lectures, as was his habit, and had simply forgotten to return it.'

There is less of a mystery about what became of 'The Disappearing Millstone,' another Hine appropriation witnessed by Ron King, who was chief clerk at Hawkins & Co. for many years. In Hitchin Historical Society's magazine *Old Hitchin Life*, he recalled:

> For many years this ancient stone, originally used for grinding corn, had rested against a brick wall in Portmill Lane... One day, as I was going to the office very early, I was horrified to see the stone fast disappearing up Portmill Lane on a stonemason's lorry. About the same time a lovely old round summerhouse or gazebo had suddenly vanished from the garden beyond our office. What could be afoot? Putting two and two together I came up with the right answer, which was confirmed a short time afterwards when I was invited [to Riddy Shott] to take tea in the garden of my old friend Reginald Hine. There was the summerhouse and there, too, forming a perfect floor to the little building was my Portmill millstone.

* * *

The historian was also an expert at persuading people to undertake research work on his behalf. As well as those acknowledged in his books, there was an unseen army of helpers – church officials, parish clerks and students of local history – who willingly responded to his appeals for help. The archive store at Hitchin Museum contains more than sixty large box files all packed with documents, notes, letters and newspaper clippings relating to the county and its people. Much of this material came from enthusiasts who were eager to contribute to the promised *History of Hertfordshire* that Hine had dreamed of writing but which never materialised. Sometimes, a request for help bordered on the bizarre, as when he was trying to solve the riddle of Henry Trigg's coffin.

During the early 18th century, when Stevenage was a small market town on the Great North Road, Henry Trigg was landlord of the Old Castle Inn. It was quite a busy hostelry, popular with passengers from the stagecoaches that stopped there to rest and change horses, and with drovers taking cattle to the London meat markets. The inn had a yard at the back containing a barn that Henry had agreed to let to the parish for use as a workhouse. However, before this arrangement could be completed the innkeeper died and the strange contents of his will, published in 1724, meant that the Parish Vestry Meeting had to start looking elsewhere for a place to house the town's Poor.

At a time when bands of nocturnal grave robbers were busy digging up newly-buried corpses to sell for anatomical research, Trigg had decided that *his* final resting place should be not in a churchyard but safely above ground in the rafters of his own barn. His will stipulated that the coffin should stay there 'upon the purlin' for thirty years, or until 'the General Resurrection when I shall receive the same again by the mighty power of God.' It seems that the body was allowed to remain there for a considerable time because Trigg's niece Anne, in a will made in 1769, left forty shillings for 'The body of my late uncle, Henry Trigg to be removed into Stevenage Churchyard from the place where he now lies, with as much privacy as possible.'

Inevitably, the coffin became one of the great curiosities of Hertfordshire. It proved a boon for successive landlords at the *Old Castle* who, for nearly two centuries, enjoyed a brisk trade from visitors who came from far and wide to see Trigg's last resting place 'halfway between Heaven and Earth.' At some time in the 1880s it was noticed that the original coffin was rotting, so to preserve his valuable source of revenue, the landlord had the lead lining (still allegedly containing the remains) transferred to a new coffin that was bound with iron bands. Hine claims that the carpenter who carried out this work took a lock of hair and a tooth from the skeleton before it was transferred – 'just to satisfy himself, and all others whom it might concern, that Trigg was still above ground.' Then came the time when the historian had to satisfy his own curiosity about the coffin's contents. It was at this point that a young newspaper reporter named Don Hills found himself sent on a necrophilic assignment that he would never forget.

By the 1940s, the inn had closed down and, throughout World War II, the building served as a Forces' Canteen run by the Women's Voluntary Service. It later became a branch of what is now the NatWest Bank. During the war years, as he was putting the finishing touches to his *Confessions*, Hine asked his friend Ernest Hodson, editor of the *Hertfordshire Express*, if he would send one of his reporters to confirm once and for all whether or not Trigg's skeleton was still inside the coffin. Having been deputed to undertake this grisly piece of research Don set off:

> Having obtained permission from the bank's manager, I climbed up into the roof of the barn and crawled across the rafters to the coffin. I found the lid was still firmly sealed but noticed that the wood at the foot of the coffin had rotted. So I knocked out the end and put my hand inside. As I was groping around I touched something soft. It turned out to be a muslin bag containing a number of bones. I took these to Mr Hine and he declared them to be animal remains.

A few weeks after Don had been recounting his story, a remarkable coincidence enabled him to slip the last piece of the puzzle into place. By chance, the two of us met at a concert at The Queen Mother Theatre in Hitchin. During the interval, Don hurried across to me. 'You're never going to believe this,' he said, 'but I've just met the person who put those bones in Trigg's coffin!' He then introduced Alfred Stokes, of Sandy in Bedfordshire, who promptly launched into the story of a schoolboy prank perpetrated back in 1928:

> I was 10 years old and one of a family of eight children living in Baker Street not far from Trigg's barn. One day my friend and

I decided to find out if there really was a skeleton inside, so we climbed up onto the rafters and discovered that both ends of the coffin had been knocked out. So I was actually able to crawl through it. All I found was an empty muslin bag. Boys being boys, we went down to Mr Shepherd the butcher and begged some bones from him – I think they were sheep bones – so we put them in the bag and went back to the barn and put the bag back in the coffin. My pal and I never told a soul because we were both scared of getting into trouble. This is the first time I've told anyone about it – and its taken me more than seventy-five years to pluck up the courage!

Never one to allow facts to spoil a good story, Hine apparently decided to ignore Don Hill's original discovery. 'It has been an open question in Stevenage whether Ann Trigg's executors did remove the body,' he wrote, 'but the coffin remained (and still remains, 1944) on the cross-beams, and I believe the body to be within ... I hope it may not be disturbed, for the wishes of any deceased should be respected.' The plain fact is that nobody knows for sure what became of the real remains of Henry Trigg. If they were re-interred elsewhere in hallowed ground, no record has been found. There are unconfirmed stories that soldiers billeted in Stevenage during the Great War broke open the coffin and took the bones as souvenirs. Whatever the case, its somewhat macabre fame has ensured that Trigg's barn is now a protected building. As for the coffin itself, a Mark III or possibly Mark IV version is now sitting up on the rafters [*Illus.* 44]. In 1999, while the building was being restored, the coffin itself was taken to the workshops of the undertaker John Austin and given a face-lift. The rotting wooden cover was removed and the original lead lining encased in another replica, thereby ensuring that the unearthly story of Henry Trigg survives into another century.

* * *

Perhaps the most entertaining of all the surreal stories touching Hine is the one that began on a Wednesday afternoon in 1907, when two young men set off to hike from Hitchin to Langley, a hamlet on the southern outskirts of the parish. They both carried knapsacks containing, among other items, a camera, photographic plates and a collapsible wooden tripod. After a couple of miles they reached the *Royal Oak* public house at Chapelfoot where they left the main road and headed off up a track towards the hilltop ruin of Minsden Chapel. Their mission was an unusual one. They were planning to photograph a ghost, the hooded apparition of a murdered nun who was said to have alarmed a number of visitors over the years with her habit of drifting in and out of the stonework. The photograph the young men obtained that day became the topic of a minor national debate that lasted on and off for twenty years, not least because it was given a measure of credibility in *The History of Hitchin*.

In his chapter on Minsden Chapel the historian writes: 'On All Hallows Eve a few years ago, a number of earnest people visited the ruins at midnight to see if haply they could surprise the Minsden ghost, the cowled apparition whose form can be faintly discerned in the photograph that fronts this page ...' And there she is [*Illus.* 46]. A transparent, veiled figure apparently emerging from the wall of the ruin. There is no explanation how the picture came to be taken; only that it is 'From a photograph by T.W. Latchmore, 1907.' We are left to assess our own level of gullibility and make of it what we will.

One thing is certain, if Reggie Hine is able to surf the web from his present location he will be chuckling over the fact that the story is still taken very seriously in some circles. Type the words *Minsden Chapel* into the search engine of any computer and you will be presented with a host of stories about spooky visits to the ruins, most of which appear to have been inspired by the photograph in Hine's book. Yet, having given it such prominence at the time, the author never mentioned the Minsden Ghost again. This is strange because, if ever there was a yarn that was tailor-made for inclusion in his *Confessions*, this is it. The McEwen brothers have always believed that their grandfather published the photograph purely as a joke, not expecting anyone to take it seriously. On the other hand, there are those who think that, because of his fascination with the paranormal, the historian had been taken in by the hoax. Like most ghost hunters, he *wanted* to believe it. There is, however, a third and far more likely theory. Namely, that the 'veiled apparition' in Latchmore's photograph is none other than Hine himself.

Thomas William (Bill) Latchmore and Hine became firm friends when they were in their early twenties. Bill's father, T.B.Latchmore, had founded their photographic business in 1865 and, over a period of seventy-five years, father and son built up a priceless pictorial record of the market town and its inhabitants. Bill, who eventually took over the business following his father's death in 1908, was always keen to try out new camera techniques and was among the first in the area to experiment with colour photography. Hine greatly admired the work of both men and used many of their photographs to illustrate his books.

Their favourite day of the week was Wednesday, when early closing meant that they could go for long afternoon walks together. Hine wrote later in his friend's obituary: 'I am thinking of the rambles that I and so many others shared with him. We would set out on one of those Hertfordshire lanes that seem to lead nowhere. But *he* knew, and by some cunning, devious route he would guide one back, even in the dark, another way.' It could well have been on one of those walks that the Minsden Ghost caper was hatched. After all, it was about this time that another prank involving a 'Roman Urn' was played upon the archaeologist George Aylott.

Curiously, it was Mr Aylott's daughter who was to supply the next link in this story, when she produced the only known surviving record of Bill Latchmore's confession that his ghost photograph was a fake. In March 1930, only a few months after the photograph had appeared in his book, Hine received a letter from Saskatchewan. It was from a Mrs David Jones, who introduced herself as the daughter of the late George Aylott. Mrs Jones, who had emigrated to Canada shortly after her marriage, enclosed a cutting from a recent edition of *American Weekly*, a Chicago-based newspaper in which the Latchmore photograph was prominently displayed beneath a banner headline proclaiming:

The Truth at last about the Famous Ghost of Minsden
The Astonishing Photograph of the Spook Which
Has Stirred Much Discussion in England, is now Explained

With the photograph was an article by Elliott O'Donnell (1872-1965), a well-known writer on the occult, who lived at Guilsborough, in Northamptonshire. He described how he first went to interview Latchmore in 1923 after hearing about the photograph from a friend. Latchmore showed it to him, explaining that he had been at Minsden that day simply to take some new pictures of the ruins for his file. 'I noticed nothing unusual at the time,' he told O'Donnell. 'It was only when I was back in my studio developing the plates that I noticed this strange image on one of them. I do not claim it is a ghost. It may only be due to some freak of light and shade, but it is extraordinary, is it not?'

O'Donnell agreed and, clearly believing he was on to a great story, set about planning a night visit to the ruins in the hope of capturing a similar photograph of the spectre. And so, on October 31st 1923 (Hallowe'en Night) a party set out from Hitchin to walk to the ruins. It was a motley group. No fewer than three representatives of the *Daily Express* (to whom, presumably, O'Donnell had sold the story), an unnamed schoolmaster, Latchmore and a lady named Mrs Everett, who reputedly had psychic powers. What follows is an extract from O'Donnell's account of their comical adventure, as published in *American Weekly* in March 1930:

> We arrived at Minsden Wood shortly before midnight ... I wanted my companions to separate, in order to perform the spells appropriate for the occasion and in the working of which Mrs Everett was an expert. She had brought with her a witch's costume which she had donned before leaving Hitchin, and its effect on the few people we had passed on our way to the ruins had been electrical. Nothing, however, would induce the newspapermen to separate, and they all remained huddled together under one of the arches, waiting with bated breath for whatever might happen.

Nothing daunted, Mrs Everett sat on the cold, damp soil and kept up a dismal chanting which was well calculated to draw even the most bashful of All Hallowe'en ghosts from its lair.

Nothing came, however, and we were all beginning to despair of experiencing any phenomenon when suddenly one of our number, with a loud ejaculation, pointed to a white light shimmering through the naked branches of a tree. 'It's come at last,' someone whispered and, on advancing toward the tree, all agog with excitement and awe, we saw what looked like a figure clad in the white costume of a nun standing in the centre of one of the arches. Our camera was at once directed towards it and, doubtless, some of us were anticipating the taking of a picture that would thrill the world. For my own part, I had doubts when someone suggested it might be an illusion of the moonlight; and so, to our intense disappointment, it proved to be naught, so far was we could judge, but a curious and distinctly eerie effect of moonbeams and shadow. It was the only thing approaching a ghost that we saw and, when 4 a.m. arrived, we decided to vacate the grove agreeing that, if it was not haunted, it ought to be, for a more eerie spot none of us had ever been in.

Tramping wearily along the high road, which was now shrouded in fog, we were startled by flashlamps being shone on us and the stentorian voices of four members of the Hertfordshire Police, bidding us to halt in the name of the law. It then transpired that the booking office at the Welwyn railway station (a few miles distant) had been broken into some hours previously and a shot fired at an official, and the police wanted to know what we were doing prowling about the highroad this early in the morning. My explanation that we were looking for a ghost produced peals of satirical laughter and a search was forthwith commenced to see if we possessed firearms. However, as luck would have it, for one of us did happen to have a revolver on him, the search was cut short by the opportune arrival of Mr Latchmore. Having the lady of our party to look after, he had not been able to keep up with us, and his corroboration of our ghost story resulted in our immediate release. Thus ended my first expedition to the haunted ruins.

Undaunted, O'Donnell decided to arrange a second Hallowe'en visit two years later in 1925, no longer accompanied by Mrs Everett in her witch's costume but by 'a stalwart Colonel and two friends.' On this occasion, it seems, other practical jokers were lying in wait, because the party's arrival at Minsden was heralded by a spectacular display of pyrotechnics:

> We had barely arrived amid the ruins before there was an explosion under our very noses, and a sudden blaze of white light., Magnesium wire! Hoaxers! The Colonel gripped tight hold of his stout ash cudgel. A few minutes later, more explosions and more lights, first in one part of the ruins and then in another. Led by the Colonel who, cudgel in hand made a rush forward, we ran to a spot among the ruins from whence the loud explosions had proceeded, and there we found a white sheet on the ground, with one end fashioned like a hood. Feeling that nothing further was likely to occur that night we returned home, the Colonel disappointed that he had not been in time to give the wearer of the sheet the cudgelling he so richly deserved.

In 1930, Latchmore decided that the hoax had gone on long enough. So he gave the persistent O'Donnell the second exclusive interview that he had been after for years. In this he admitted for the first time that the image was not photographed accidentally, as he had first claimed, but as the result of a carefully planned experiment. He had read of a new method of taking such photographs and, to test it, he arranged with his friend to visit Minsden Chapel. The friend put on a hooded sheet and posed for a timed exposure in front of the ruin. Then Latchmore closed the shutter, the friend withdrew and the exposure was completed, producing the effect of the ghost. But when it came to O'Donnell's final question 'And who was the ghost that you photographed that day?' Bill Latchmore would not be drawn. 'I can say only that it was a friend,' he replied. 'We agreed at the time that I should never disclose his name. All I *can* say is that the figure was intended as the personification of the ghostly nun who is supposed to haunt Minsden.'

When Hine first published the Minsden ghost photograph readers were surprised to learn that he had effectively become the owner of the ruin. 'Is there any other attorney I wonder who has a fourteenth-century church belonging to him?' he wrote. 'There I do claim to be uncommon. True it is only for the term of my natural life, by lease from the vicars of Hitchin, but as I intend that my body or ashes shall be laid to rest in the chancel I have more than a tenant's quiet enjoyment. I have enlarged my title and usurped a freeholder's pride of ownership.' So the reason that he chose not to reveal the truth about the ghostly photograph could have been because, quite simply, he wished to preserve the atmosphere of mystery that he and others have been able to sense on their visits to the ruins:

> Minsden is for those, rather, whose *minds* are in ruins; for those sons of quietness who are distracted by the crimes and follies and misfortunes of mankind. In its deep shade many who have been brought low by the cares of this world, or in my case the wear and tear of my profession, have found healing, consolation and repose ... the very air at Minsden is tremulous with that faint *susurrus* – call it the undersong of the earth, the music of the spheres, the sigh of departed time or what you will – which only the more finely attuned spirits overhear.

It would be interesting to know whether Hine was aware of the work of Alfred Watkins (1855-1935) a Herefordshire businessman who in the 1920s introduced the modern world to the controversial subject of ley lines. Leys are based on the theory that our Stone Age forebears were far more intelligent and in tune with their environment than we give them credit for. That the spots where they chose to build their stone circles, burial chambers and other sacred sites are, in fact, aligned with one another on carefully chosen tracks that seem to contain some unexplained force or energy.

To present-day pagans the strongest and most important ley in Britain is the invisible line that traces the path of the sunrise on May Day. This line traverses southern England from Norfolk down to St Michael's Mount in Cornwall and includes in its path such prominent prehistoric sites as Glastonbury and the Avebury stone circle. Interestingly, as the line crosses Hertfordshire, it touches both Royston Cave (the mysterious mediaeval bell chamber beneath the town's crossroads) and – yes – the ruins of Minsden Chapel. Knowing now that a large number of early Christian churches were deliberately built on pagan sites in order to obliterate them, is it possible that Minsden was such a site in pre-Christian times? Only an archaeological excavation would determine that. Meanwhile, there is a growing theory among students of the supernatural that the ruins, while not haunted in the general sense of the word, do contain a 'presence' of some kind; a force that some have found restorative and others disturbing.

[8]
'A Personal Impression'

IN ONE SENSE this chapter could be regarded as an interlude in Hine's life story because it is not really about *him*. Rather, it is about others as he remembered them. A miscellany of observations on the lives of a handful of men, some of who might have been granted immortality in one of his books had the promised second edition of *Worthies* ever been published. Instead, these eulogies took the form of either a private letter or a tribute published in the local newspaper. 'At the risk of becoming a professional necrologist,' Hine wrote, 'I have composed many personal impressions and character sketches of my client-friends to supplement the formal obituary notices printed in local papers. So many of them have deserved a good remembrance, and of the last sad offices it is the one I have liked best to do.'

These pen portraits were not commissioned; they were written only if Hine felt moved to write them. Some are such a pleasure to read that one can almost sense the warm glow of pride felt by the bereaved when they opened their local newspaper to discover that their loved one had earned *two* obituaries, one carrying the prestigious byline: 'A Personal Impression by Reginald L. Hine, F.S.A.'

Thomas William Latchmore
(1882-1946)

Here, the historian pays homage to his photographer friend and fellow practical joker Bill Latchmore, though regrettably he makes no mention of their Minsden ghost prank. When Latchmore died in September 1946 he was living alone in rooms that were part of his photographic studios at the corner of Brand Street and Paynes Park, Hitchin. The studio itself was in the roof of 11 Brand Street, the building that Latchmore's father, Thomas Benwell Latchmore, had bought in 1870. It was from here that father and son ran their photographic business for three-quarters of a century. As Hine's tribute suggests, the business and the property had gone into decline some time before Latchmore's sudden death, at the age of sixty-four:

> Such is the hot pace of this present life that one has not a moment to spare for those who have fallen by the wayside or to reflect coolly and calmly upon what the loss of them means to us who are still in the flesh and travelling or rather tearing on. Those who can pause will miss Latchmore's familiar figure, with his dog – the by no means spotless Spot – in and about the streets of Hitchin and, on his longed-for Wednesday afternoons, far afield.
>
> Some of us will curse the fell sergeant Death for filching away the one man who was a mine of information on the folklore, topography and archaeology of these parts. Himself, he did not care over much to help; but he was a devoted servant of the sons of learning. When people came to me with coins that they had found 'Latchmore is the man,' I always replied. 'He will date them for you.' So with flint implements, Samian and Belgic pottery, mediaeval ironwork, place-names, field-names, bridle-ways, footpaths and earthworks.
>
> Here was no narrow blear-eyed specialist; he was in mind as in figure rotund and widely equipped. I am thinking of the rambles that I and so many others shared with him. We would set out on one of those Hertfordshire lanes that seem to lead to nowhere. But *he* knew, and by some cunning, devious route, he would guide one back, even in the dark, another way. So likewise in the byways of knowledge. He was always exploring, venturing a little further into the unknown. This week I was to have gone to three lectures with him and to two libraries. That information-mine of his, however much the others dug into it, was always filling up.
>
> Inevitably he had the defects of a good quality. He accumulated too much. If he lectured on 'The Icknield Way' or 'The Village of Pirton' or his holidays in Wales he could never make an end. Each sentence, each slide, beguiled him into a dissertation, and many of his 'asides' would have made fascinating lectures in themselves. So with his novel with which I wrestled long. It was crammed with

folk-lore, gipsy-lore and with the eccentrics and village characters of these parts. But the story was lost in a welter of words and wanderings. I doubt if ever it will find its way into print.

So with his rooms. I visited him there a few hours before his death. In the miscalled sitting room there was nowhere to sit. He had one chair. Spot had the other. I stood. Round about, cluttering the walls and the floor and the tables, were books and papers and files, the debris of a lifetime collecting of a bachelor bibliophile. 'You'll be just like Hazlitt,' I remarked. 'Do you remember he filled up every room in the house with books and at last was obliged to sleep on the stairs?' He smiled and queried, 'Am I really as hopeless as that?'

And now, instead, he will sleep too soundly in six feet of Hitchin soil within the town he loved so well. That is right and fitting, for he adored the place of his birth. In their time he and his father had done what they could to save it from being despoiled by the Philistines, and when venerable buildings simply had to go, the Latchmores not merely took but made photographs to record and perpetuate their memory. How fortunate have I been to be able to use their work – nay, their loving labour, in the books that I have written. Latchmore had many friends. But the closest and dearest was his dog. Spot has already gone to hunt for his master and I shall desperately hope that they may discover 'footpaths to felicity' in a better world.

Within a few years of Latchmore's death, 11 Brand Street itself joined the ranks of 'venerable buildings that simply had to go' and was demolished to make way for *Latchmore Court*, one of the better examples of 20th century commercial architecture that now graces our town. The fate that befell the contents of the old Latchmore building is a more disturbing story. In common with too many of their contemporaries, neither Thomas Latchmore nor his son took any steps to ensure that their life's work was preserved for posterity. At the time of Bill's death there were in his house several hundred glass plate negatives dating back to the first, taken by his father in the 1860s. 'Few towns possess such a priceless pictorial record of the past,' the journalist Reg Cannon wrote. 'A record which marks growth and sweeping changes in landmarks and in the fashions and habits of its people.'

A few days after his story was published Cannon received an urgent telephone call from a friend whose office overlooked the back yard of the Latchmore studios. He hurried round and was horrified to discover that workmen had been sent in with orders to empty the property and were throwing all the glass negatives from an upstairs window into the back of a lorry. Only six were recovered intact. Had this not happened, there is a chance that Hitchin would now have a Latchmore Gallery akin to the fabulous Frank Sutcliffe Gallery at Whitby in North Yorkshire, where a shop honouring the town's pioneer photographer does brisk business selling reproductions of his work.

As it is, we are much indebted to those curators and staff at Hitchin Museum who, over the past half-century, have worked hard to build up a respectable collection of Latchmore photographs from numerous private sources. Perhaps one day their efforts will be further rewarded. At the time of the house clearance four large albums of original photographs disappeared. All carefully annotated they represented the life's work of father and son. So far they have not been traced. If they are still intact, it is to be hoped that one day these priceless records will be shared with the rest of the community and handed over to the town museum where, surely, they rightly belong.

Ralph Erskine Sanders
(1851-1933)

One small but important part of the Latchmore collection that did survive is their record of the arrival of the motor car in Hitchin. The company that made the wooden bodies for these vehicles was that of Ralph E. Sanders, whose long life bridged the years that saw the gradual transition from horse power to the internal combustion engine. Born at Buntingford in 1851, Sanders had been apprenticed into his father's trade of coach maker and opened his own business in Royston, in 1876. As a craftsman whose work depended upon a steady supply of high quality wood, he became one of East Anglia's most respected experts on English timber. His ability to accurately 'cube up' and value standing trees, more or less at a glance, put him in great demand at estate timber sales.

In 1898 Ralph extended his business to Hitchin when his company bought out the Odell Brothers carriage building works in Bridge Street. He also purchased a strip of land in Walsworth Road, where he erected the town's first purpose-built motor garage. Although never very fond of mechanically propelled vehicles, Sanders was astute enough to realise that they would eventually replace the phaetons, traps and dog carts of his generation. So it was in the Sanders workshops that Bill Latchmore was able to capture scenes that provide a fascinating illustration of those few years preceding the assembly line era, when the car bodies were still being built of wood alongside the horse drawn carriages they were slowly replacing [*Illus.* 47 & 48].

As an articled clerk with Hawkins & Co. Hine had much to do with Ralph Sanders' business affairs. Later, he witnessed the further growth of the company as the sons built it up into one of the leading motor agencies of the county. When the founder died in 1933 Hine wrote a lengthy tribute that appeared in the *Royston Crow* in Ralph Sanders' hometown. Here is part of it:

One by one, the eccentrics have departed, but there are still a few men left amongst us whose strong and masterful traits stand out from the monotonous level of tamed humanity. Ralph Erskine Sanders was one of these. Like many other able and successful men of an earlier age, he was an Original, almost a Character. A fine piece of timber in the rough, so you might fairly style him, with no veneer, no finish in his make-up, though the coaches and 'bodies' he built lacked nothing in that way.

It is the dynamic energy of such men that one admires. One felt, and certainly he knew, that he was predestined to succeed. But his was no easy success. Early and late, single minded and incessantly, he was at his work of making money, and of enlarging the business and the fortunes of the family he founded. Leisure he had none, he laboured without remission. To sit down in a chair was impossible to him. If you watched him in his own home, he would be pacing up and down the room, thinking, planning for the morrow. To bed soon after nine, he would be up at dawn and do half an ordinary man's work before it was time to breakfast. So many of us tired mortals are slaves to sleep, 'wherein almost half the life-time of man creepeth away'; but this indomitable man, hard as teak in his constitution, could do with precious little. He once quoted a saying I had not heard before: 'The right time to begin gardening is the year before last,' and with a pull at his pipe he then added: 'The right time to begin the day's business is to begin before the day.'

I used to think him dangerously impulsive in his business dealings. He would buy a whole forest of timber or a largish estate without, apparently, a moment's hesitation. He allowed his eldest son (Frank) twenty minutes' notice before taking him off to Hitchin to be apprenticed. He bought Odell's coach building business in Bridge-street, Hitchin, in a casual five-minute talk, just as if he were buying a coat across a counter. But there was a lifetime of experience behind his every impulse and also, as I fancy, that sixth sense that makes for success.

Off his beaten track, his second thoughts, not his first, were best; and if you were patient with him, you could generally depend upon them working in your favour. Readers of this paper will remember how (almost without thinking) he outraged the feelings of the Cottered people by cutting down a tree called 'Bumpy' which, 'like some great prelate of the grove' had stood from time immemorial, and had been almost worshipped upon Cottered village green. Mr Sanders, as Lord of the Manor, might have chosen to justify his action in the courts, but he chose rather to appear before the Parish Council, and there and then made a voluntary gift of the village green to Cottered forever.

The study of human beings is fascinating, because it is full of surprises. Here was a man with a character seemingly as hard as nails, and, as I told him, he 'generally had a wasp in his bonnet.' But no needle is sharp at both ends, and this self-centred and sharp man undoubtedly possessed a softer side. I wish he had shown it more. Not merely once, but on several occasions, he extracted the uttermost farthing from some recalcitrant debtor and then, after a month, instructed me to send the money back.

One liked him also because he had not been spoilt by success. Though he became what you may call a well-to-do man, it made no difference to the simple order and disposition of his life. In a world that grows, almost daily, more concerned about its personal appearance, he went about shabby and unconcerned. Two years ago I chaffingly asked him to let me have his old overcoat for our projected Hitchin Museum. He smiled and said he would consider it in his will but that, meantime, he found it comfortable. In other respects he was singular. He never wore a pair of shoes or even a pair of laced boots. He insisted upon button boots, though they had long since gone out of fashion.

As a countryman, he had a natural instinct for the land. It meant something to him. It was *real* estate in the true sense of that word. In this transitory world he had seen so many things disappear; even coaches and coach building had had their day and ceased to be. But land was not unreal; though it might decline in value, it couldn't run away, and you could leave it to your sons and daughters after you were dead and gone. A short while before he died he was heard muttering to himself as he strode over one of his farms: 'All mine, all mine.' Not in sense vaingloriously or madly possessed by his own property, but with a countryman's proper pride in having acquired these broad acres by the sweat of his own brow, by his unaided industry and business acumen.

When Shakespeare made money, he followed a similar instinct and bought land at Stratford-on-Avon. To Sanders Shakespeare ranked next to (and indeed almost equal with) God. He was a close reader of the plays, but he was more than a reader, he was a devourer of them. He had no necessity to read. Scenes, acts and entire plays were, from his youth up, fixed in his memory forever. Often in my office he would leave bickering about mortgages, leases and contracts and (blessed relief) we would have Buckingham's valedictory speech out of *Henry the Eighth* or Lear's terrific 'Blow winds and crack your cheeks ...' and perhaps a dozen passages more, winding up, a little cruelly sometimes, with Dick the Butcher's threat: 'The first thing we'll do, lets kill all the lawyers.' Perhaps we wasted a lot of hours that way, but he was the better for it, and I don't think he would have demurred later, if he had discovered in our bill of costs: 'To discussing with you the finer points of *Timon of Athens*, 6s 8d.' He was never cantankerous about lawyers' bills.

His other book was the Bible, the noble Authorised Version which was printed in the year that Shakespeare gave up writing plays (1611). Certainly, in the Old Testament, Sanders was deeply and reverently read. It pleases me that his last wish was to hear the first Psalm read, for there is a verse of promise in that Psalm which must have comforted and lifted up his heart:

'And he shall be like a tree, planted by the rivers of water,
That bringeth forth his fruit in his season;
His leaf also shall not wither
And whatsoever he doeth shall prosper.'

F. L. Griggs, R.A.
(1876 - 1938)

The etcher and draughtsman Frederick Landseer Griggs was one of England's finest architectural artists of the early 20th century. His sketches, engravings and prints are sought the world over, and one of the largest collections, containing more than twenty of his best works, is now owned by the Fine Arts Museums of San Francisco. The son of a High Street baker, Griggs was born and educated in Hitchin. He and Hine became firm friends and throughout their younger days 'coupled as hounds together' they delighted in hunting down the lost works of Hertfordshire's early artists. Hine wrote of him later: 'His heart – like his religion – was staked firmly and far back in the Middle Ages. It was there he found the best craft work, the beauty, simplicity and piety of life – cities and towns and churches just as they should be.'

In 1900 Griggs was commissioned by the publisher Sir Frederick Macmillan (who then lived near Hitchin at Temple Dinsley) to illustrate a new series of countryside books that his firm was planning to publish under the general title of *Highways and Byways*. The series was a runaway success and provided the artist with a source of income for the rest of his life. While travelling the country to make his sketches Griggs visited and fell in love with the beautiful Gloucestershire market town of Chipping Campden. In 1906, to Hine's dismay, he decided to settle there; but not before he had made numerous drawings of the Hertfordshire countryside in which he had grown up. Some of these Hine later put to good use in his book *Charles Lamb & his Hertfordshire*.

So far as Griggs was concerned, the architectural ruination of his birth town began when the historic houses of Bancroft – 'one of the most beautiful streets in England'– started to fall into the hands of traders, who promptly turned them into shops. Eventually, he became so disenchanted with the changes that he stopped coming to Hitchin and concentrated his energies on the preservation of his new and prettier hometown in the Cotswolds. However, in 1936 Hine persuaded the artist to return for one night only to deliver what turned out to be a valedictory lecture about the town he remembered from his youth. It was Griggs' last visit before his death.

Hine arranged for the talk to be published as a booklet entitled *An Artists Looks at Hitchin*. He included in it extracts from an unpublished memoir of Griggs. The extracts reveal something of the nostalgic sadness felt by this important artist during the last years of his life:

> His chief pleasure was to make up a side of good fellows in an old-fashioned inn, and get them garrulous about the past. There would be some leg-pulling (at which he was an adept, watching one intently to see just how far it was safe to go) some banter and some priceless unexpurgated stories. The sad thing about his own stories is that they never reached their end. One is left wondering unto this day. They must have been brilliant, but about two-thirds of the way through, when one was hopeful that the climax was in sight, he would be attacked by a spasm of self-contained and private merriment. Ripples of jocularity would run over his droll face;

then something more extravagantly comic would take him by the throat, depriving him of speech as, from top to toe, he was doubled up with delight, shaking and writhing in paroxysms of resounding Gargantuan laughter. One could not laugh at his story; one simply laughed at Griggs.

When a man laughs like that there may be something amiss. Often I suspected that his laughter was, at heart, no laughing matter. Some men have to go on jesting lest their hearts should break . . . Sitting in an inn, with boon companions about him and a tankard of black-cap cider – 'very pretty drinking' – at his elbow, Griggs could keep dark thoughts at bay. But, so often as he left the snug and friendly place, the desecration of the street outside would strike him like a coward's blow...

Every year he grew more disconsolate about the changes – all for the worse – in his 'dear, detestable Hitchin.' He vowed that he would never look by daylight upon the local Philistines and their vandalistic works. All he would do was to come to me at Riddy Shott by night, go like a mourner about the vulgarised and plate-glassed streets, and be off again at dawn. Nothing could utterly destroy his wistful and tender regard for the place where he was born. But his affection was for things that are no more seen. It was for the Hitchin, truly imagined, of the Middle Ages; for the royal and ancient manor as it was in Stuart and Georgian times. Yes, and for the still unspoilt market and country town of his own boyhood ... So we went to *The Sun* by night, dined and drank there with sundry boon-companions, tapping their vintage memories. And so on to Church House where, to a sober and respectable audience, his lecture was delivered ... They are gallant men who fight on for the preservation of rural England, and the regeneration of its towns: all the more gallant because they fight a losing battle. Griggs contested every inch of the ground; but it broke his heart, and he was on the point of capitulating even at Campden when the summons came to die.

21. An early 20th-century view of Hitchin's main street, Bancroft, showing the entrance to Portmill Lane on the right.

22. Portmill Lane with the offices of Hawkins & Co. halfway down on the left.

23. 'My father-in-the-law.' The solicitor W. O. Times

24. The architect's sketch of Riddy Shott, the Hines' home in Wymondley Road, Hitchin from 1917-1929.

Within the sketch:

HOUSE AT HITCHEN·
GEOFFRY LUCAS·ARCHT·

25. R.H. relaxing on the terrace with his daughter Felicity in 1925

26. R.H. at work in the attic study at Riddy Shott, 1927

27. An early passport …

28. … in which the articled clerk promoted himself.

29. 1936. Members of Hitchin Oddfellows hear from R.H. how Cromwell's army tore down statues of the saints from the south porch of St Mary's Church during the Civil War.

30. Florence, in the uniform of District Commissioner for Guides, at the wheel of her Crossley sports car in 1934.

31. An eviction from one of the 'squalid quarrelsome underworld of little yards' that was part of Hitchin's Queen Street slum area in 1904. On the left, the formidable figure of Police Superintendent John Reynolds.

32. St Mary's Square in the early 1930s shortly after the slum clearance and completion of the River Hiz improvement scheme.

33. The partners and staff of Hawkins & Co. in 1932. Hine is standing on the left. The senior partners, Major Wilberforce Times and Arthur Linsdell are seated, second and fourth from the left respectively.

IN ANGELLIS

CUM LIBELLIS

EX LIBRIS

REGINALD L. HINE.

34. Hine's personal bookplate. The Latin inscription reads 'To be with books is to be among angels' or more simply 'Books are heaven'.

35. Felicity Hine's actor friend, Michael Hordern, climbed an elm tree to obtain this 'aerial' view of Willian Bury in 1936.

36. Hordern (*standing centre*) and Felicity (*right*, in the 'Principal Boy' pose) when they appeared together in *As You Like It* at Hitchin Priory.

37. Felicity Hine's wedding to Bill McEwen in 1938. Her parents are standing behind her. Bill's are on the right of the picture.

38. The bride arriving at All Saints' Church, Willian

39. Bill McEwen with his first son, Andrew, in 1942.

40 - 41. The novelist Ursula Bloom (1892-1984) and a marked printer's proof of page 85 of *Confessions*, showing Hine's final corrections and the seven words that upset her – 'if ever she looks at a bill'.

42. This oil painting of Hine by Gerard Ceunis was used for the frontispiece in the first edition of *Confessions*. By the second it had been dropped …

43 … in favour of a new studio photograph by Frances Coombe.

44. Henry Trigg's coffin today, still perched in the rafters of a barn in Stevenage but with a new outer cover.

45. The ruins of Minsden Chapel in 1832, by the topographical artist J.C. Buckler, 1793-1894, one of a family of draughtsmen and architects, much employed by the antiquarians..

46. The Minsden 'ghost' apparently emerging through a wall of the ruins. The controversial photograph taken by T.W. Latchmore in 1907.

47. From carriages to cars. Ralph Sanders' coach-building workshop in Walsworth Road, Hitchin *c.*1908.

48. The finished product. An elegant wooden body on a metal chassis supplied by French engineers.

'A PERSONAL IMPRESSION'

Arthur W. Brunt
(1861 - 1946)

Arthur Brunt was a journalist and pioneer resident of Letchworth Garden City. He served as a town councillor and local magistrate but is probably best remembered as a founder and editor of the town's principal local newspaper *The Citizen*. In 1906, he took part in a printers' strike at The Garden City Press, which was then publishing the short-lived *Garden City Record & Advertising Journal*. Having been 'father of the chapel' Brunt was one of those not taken back after the dispute. So he and two others who were in a similar predicament pooled their modest resources and, with the help of advertising sponsors, set about publishing their own newspaper.

Later that year, on 22nd September 1906, the first edition of *The Citizen* hit the still muddy and largely unlit streets of the garden city. It had been produced at an improvised printing works set up in the bedroom and kitchen of a house in Green Lane, where one of the sacked employees lived. Type was set entirely by hand and printing was done on a primitive treadle machine. Every week a thousand copies were run off and distributed free to every household. Brunt, who was Advertising Manager, undertook the deliveries. He found it hazardous work during the dark winter months when much of the town was still little more than a building site.

Yet, from these precarious beginnings, the group went on to form a thriving printing company and *The Citizen* flourished as the town's main newspaper for the next seventy years. Arthur Brunt tells this story in *Pageant of Letchworth (1903-1914)*, the first book about 'ordinary people' who were involved in shaping the garden city during its early years. When it was published in 1942 the author invited Hine to write a foreword. A somewhat risky move considering the lawyer's early reputation for teasing the garden city about its lack of history. Few forgot the opening of Letchworth Museum in 1920, when he made the comment that it was 'a praiseworthy and laudable project to build a museum when

129

as yet you have nothing to put in it but yourselves.' Then, in 1925, he published a short poem:

'God the first garden made,
And the first city, Cain.'
Deep in a proverb so 'tis laid
Profound, precise and plain.
But garden cities, garden cities?
Who the deuce makes garden cities?
Will someone please explain?
It is a hundred thousand pities
They do not say in these old ditties.
For then we'd know, for weal or woe
Whence all these mad, mixed blessings flow;
And folk would be no more perplext
With that dark thought they now are vext
Is God or Man to blame?

The day after the verse had been published, Letchworth's founder, Sir Ebenezer Howard, sent Hine a post card. 'You need not blame God,' he wrote. 'If anyone it is I who am to blame. I promise to do better next time,' After which he returned to building his second garden city at Welwyn. In fact, Hine followed the development of both towns with great interest even though, like many others, he had early doubts about their future success. As the following extracts show, he produced a thoughtful piece for Brunt's book, raising a question that is still asked today, about whether a new town can ever develop the 'soul' intended by its founders:

PAGEANT OF LETCHWORTH

Throughout these pages one is continually reminded of the heart cry out of Coriolanus: 'What is the city but the people? Truly the people *are* the city.' That is rightly the keynote, the emphasis of this book, and also the delight of it in the reading; for did we not know these men? Did we not walk and talk with them? Is it not pious and proper to have their names recorded? You may build your roads and bridges, you may lay your sewers, your gas and your electric mains. You may multiply shops and pile up your rateable values. But what shall it profit a city to gain all these adjuncts of town planning and fail to acquire a soul? And what city can possess a soul unless it be inhabited by honourable men?

At Letchworth – as Mr Brunt shows – we have been singularly blessed. His own sympathies, politically and personally, lie with the common or garden men – shall we call them the under-gardeners? But here, of necessity he has to deal with the head gardeners, and of such there has been no lack. From the beginning there has been Howard's plenty. It is not that the estate was zoned for twelve good men to the acre. The explanation is that, at the outset, only men of high seriousness, his 'chosen people' rallied to Howard's call. Who else could have made the exodus out of Egypt and, like the author, would have borne the brunt of those early unpromising days, when the wilderness seemed most unlikely to blossom as the rose?

Assuredly it was a fine breed of men who followed this desperate adventure, and it is due to their example that Letchworth was dowered not merely with an intense local patriotism but a certain spirituality in its town life. Would it not be a pity, would it not seem a betrayal, if that gracious indwelling spirit departed out of our midst?

Howard's anxiety in his latter days was lest his experiment should succeed *too* well. He knew the dangers of success. Again and again I used to implore him to keep to his first intent, and limit the size of the city to that of the Greek city-states, for whose ten or fifteen thousand folk it was just possible to remain a happy family and never, by swelling numbers, to become an agglomeration of people. There are always plenty of people, I used to urge, but many a town has perished for lack of men. Does one need to point out those other perils, of overstocking the garden, of unloosening the agricultural belt?

These are problems that will increase in urgency as the population grows. But there are other problems. How to bring back the first fine frenzy of the Garden City in its youth? How to fill up the ranks of the pioneers? 'I owe my success,' declared the founder, 'to the co-operation of men far abler than myself.' Is Howard,

I wonder, still justified by the works of his disciples? How to overcome the self-satisfaction of a community that took a modest vow of poverty in its novitiate and now boasts of its ground rents and punctual dividends? How to stem the apathy of a people who, in the second generation, are inheriting this pleasant plot of earth instead of earning it by the sweat of their own brows? A book like this should make its readers think, and thought is but vanity unless it be transmuted into action. Should not this vivid pageantry of the past do something to re-arouse the public spirit of the present; reminding townspeople that, as Howard's descendants, they are not isolated individuals at liberty to follow their own ends, but fortunate citizens of no mean city and owing a common allegiance to its ideals?

Although the Brunt family has been left with the impression that Hine conducted his long friendship with Arthur 'in a slightly aloof way' the two men clearly held each other in high regard. In *Pageant of Letchworth*, the author reveals that he was one of those who had heard Hine present his first-ever paper to members of East Herts Archaeological Society at Newnham Hall in 1910. 'We knew at once that here was a writer of rare literary gifts,' he says. Aloof or not, Hine was undoubtedly sincere in his letter to the photographer and naturalist Donald Brunt, following his father's death in 1946:

Alas I only heard of the passing of your good old father on Wednesday afternoon, and just too late to pay the last (no, not sad, but joyful) offices and attend his burial. There is something more than admiration in my remembrance of him, something akin to affection, for with all his public work, *private* people – Tom, Dick and Harry – meant more to him than anything else, and his thought and his care were for individual human beings. That is evident in all his writings too. What unknown and immeasurable good he must have done (and always with right spirit) in his day and generation. And there was constantly a twinkle in his eye, a liking for unusual and eccentric character, an understanding mind in all the problems that he helped to solve. Truly, a dedicated life.

Historians have long memories and I am not likely to forget either the man or his writings. He took the chair for me at the first lecture I ever gave in Letchworth, and that is a long time ago. All the years since then I have been deepening my acquaintance into esteem and into friendship. I like to think how much his work will live on and perpetuate his memory. My wish would be not that he should rest in peace but, in a better world, meet his old friends and find new work to do.

Charles Fleming
(1873-1941)

Despite his teasing the Letchworth people over their brief past Hine was keen to help them discover the ancient history of 'the new land' to which they had come. As the contents of the town's two museums show only too well the community has enjoyed more than its share of dedicated archaeologists and historians, right up to the present day. One of the earliest was Charles Fleming, who was renowned for the lectures he gave at his home in Baldock Road. This short appreciation by Hine appeared in *The Citizen* in February 1941:

> He slipped out of life with the quiet unobtrusiveness that was so characteristic of him. One's heart is full of thinking of him; one's memory is heavily laden. Yet one writes with restraint. He would hate to have extravagant words said or any fuss made upon his departure. At least let this be said: Here was a true servant of the sons of learning, a singularly charming, warm-natured man, not merely willing but eager out of his abundance of widely-garnered knowledge to assist scholars, writers and teachers with their problems. And not a few will miss those Friday evenings at his house where, in his free and easy arm-chair manner, he would expound the history and, by his lovely photographs, display the distinctive charms of the villages and townships of this top corner of North Hertfordshire.
>
> It was I who first persuaded, or shall I say *compelled* him to

deliver lectures to somewhat larger audiences. He dubbed himself 'the world's worst speaker.' But it was precisely his 'conversation way,' free from the taint of formality or pompous phrase, that captivated his hearers. You smiled and laughed and chuckled with him for fifty minutes but towards the end you were aware that you had seen slides of marvellous quality and had been listening to a man whose knowledge of medieval England had been wide and deep.

To put him at ease, I used, whenever I took the chair for him, to let him perch upon the chairman's table (no light matter this) and puff away at his endless cigarettes. There, as I found, he would be at his best, though so often we had to wait for his troublesome coughing to clear. Alas, he loved smoking not this side but the other side of idolatry; and we must hope desperately, for his sake, that there is still such a thing as tobacco in a better world.

Ernest Squires
1878-1933

Finally, this short but evocative description of an amateur historian's study should ring a few bells with readers. Taken from a Hine monograph published in *Transactions*, the magazine of the East Herts Archaeological Society, it is dedicated to Ernest Squires of Hertford, a founder of the society and its magazine editor for many years.

As an inveterate bachelor and bibliophile, Squires refused to have himself or his belongings tidied up. There was a willing and capable maid, but she was commanded on no account to meddle with his study. It was not to be spring-cleaned or dusted till he died. If you took tea with him down in St Andrew Street he would perhaps shift a *Clutterbuck* or two to make way for the tray. But the crumpets would have to perch on a pile of *Transactions*; the three kinds of jam (generous epicure!) would squat side by side on Unwick's *Nonconformity in Hertfordshire*; and the cherry cake would entice you from Tregelles' *History of Hoddesdon*.

On the side tables, on the top of bookcases and on the floor, scattered in scholarly disarray, were the *disjecta membra* of his life as a working antiquary. Articles, proofs, tracings, rubbings, photostats, deeds, documents, pedigrees and a litter of letters from contributors, printers and friends. It was my melancholy privilege to go through these 'remains' after his death. It was then, for the first time, I learned how widely his activities ranged; how many historians and archaeologists near and far had come to him for counsel and been glad to take alms out of his open treasury of knowledge.

[9]
Friendships, Letters and
Unspoken Codes

O F ALL PLACES, it was in Hine's much-extolled parish church of St Mary that the suggestion was made that he may have been bisexual. Parishioners had been celebrating a special thanksgiving service and there was quite a crowd in the Trinity Chapel chatting noisily over a glass of wine, as one does in church these days from time to time. During the course of this jolly *après-worship* a clergyman new to the parish edged his way through the throng to introduce himself. 'Do you have any projects on at the moment?' he inquired eventually. I mentioned this biography, guessing that he had probably not yet heard of Reginald Hine. I was wrong. 'Ah,' he replied. 'Hitchin's gay historian.' As definitions go, that was a first. When I inquired how he had reached this conclusion he said simply: 'Well, I'm reading his books and it seems to be there in his writing'.

It has to be said that similar thoughts passed through my own mind from time to time. The first occasion was after reading Hine's enthusiastic description of the schoolboy crush on his English master that had lasted throughout his life. There are also his accounts of 'chance' meetings – in the street and in bookshops – with older men who were later to influence his life. One wonders, also, how many readers harboured similar suspicions after learning of Hine's long-term relationship with his bachelor employer – 'my intimate friend of thirty-four years' – Onslow Times. For a long while I had strong reservations about whether it was at all necessary to air these suspicions when there is no evidence whatever to support them. No letters, no diaries. However, the very fact that the historian's writing can, itself, put the question in a reader's mind suggests that the clergyman's theory should at least be discussed.

There is a teasing sentence in a letter written to James Curry shortly before *Confessions of An Un-Common Attorney* was published. 'The best is there,' Hine promised, 'though much lies slyly hiding between the lines for discerning readers like yourself to decipher.' Why should an historian of all people wish to hide things between the lines? Written in 1944 when homosexuality was still 'the love that dare not speak its name' could it be that the book contains some of those hidden pointers that gay writers liked to slip in for the benefit of readers of a similar bent? Should we attach any significance to the lawyer's penchant for bowls of *pot-pourri* in his study and office and his whimsical choice of attire, flaunted throughout what must have been the dreariest period *ever* in the history of male fashion?

Audrey Farr, a secretary at Hartley & Hine during the post-war years, remembered: 'I have seen him greet men with a kiss on the cheek, which I suppose was unusual in the 1940s. But we just thought – "Well, *that's* Mr Hine." There was also the parting observation of Ina Roberts, when recalling their tennis party days: 'Only when I was older did I realise what a quaint fish he was. My abiding memory of Reggie is seeing him and Onslow Times walking together along the High Street with their arms around each other.' Although such behaviour may have raised a few homophobic eyebrows in a small country town in the 1920s, it was not at all uncommon among the people that Hine admired. With the writers and artists of the Bloomsbury Group, whose lectures he attended frequently, it was common practice for the heartiest of heterosexual men to greet each other with a kiss on both cheeks and walk arm-in-arm through the streets of W.C.1. And let us not forget his great love of the Italian people and their way of life; a country where, for centuries, any man not greeting a male relation or a *compare* with a kiss on both cheeks would be considered a bit of a cold fish.

The 'gay historian' theory does not ring true with any of Hine's three grandsons, although Andrew McEwen says he can understand how people might gain that impression from reading his books. 'Had it been true. I think we would have heard at least a hint of it,' was his conclusion. 'Nothing that my grandmother, mother or father ever said pointed in that direction. While my grandmother and mother would have been reticent on such a private matter I am sure my father would have told me. Both my wife and I feel that, had my grandfather been gay, my grandmother would have left him. She was most definitely *not* the sort of person who would have accepted such a situation.'

Perhaps the answer is to be found in the down side of Hine's life; in his ongoing anxiety over health problems, in the nightmares and the insomnia. It is more likely that his rather camp exuberance served as a shield, behind which hid an acutely sensitive man who preferred the safety of celibacy and platonic friendships to the powerful emotions of physical intimacy. As his grandson put it: 'It is possible that all the passion in his soul was channelled into his writing – that producing a well-turned phrase gave him far more pleasure than any physical bond.' This could be the reason that women of all ages found him so attractive. 'Hitchin's perfect gentleman,' was how one described him. A highly personable, good-looking chap who cut a dashing figure but at the same time presented no physical threat. Courteous and witty yet somewhat aloof. Everything, in fact, that fascinates a woman.

Only in one place did any of Hine's lady friends admit to feeling threatened, and that was when they accepted a lift in his car. He was, by his own admission, an appalling driver. His bone-shaking Austin 7 saloon (*circa* 1929) was known affectionately as *Sir Henry* in homage to Sir Henry Chauncy, whose 18th-century epic *The Historical Antiquities of Hertfordshire* had first stirred the young Hine's interest in local history. It was the real Sir Henry who had helped indirectly to pay for the machine. In 1928 Hine had managed to acquire part of the original manuscript for this book. A few years later, in need of some cash, he sold it to the person then living in Chauncy's old home, Ardeley Bury. Hine doesn't reveal how much money changed hands, only that it helped to clear some debts 'and paid for a car, which I named *Sir Henry.*'

Sadly, there is no surviving photograph of this famous old crock, the only car Hine ever owned. As the vehicle itself deteriorated into a rather forlorn antiquity, the workshop foreman at Sanders' garage would plead with him to buy another and allow *Sir Henry* to conk out in quiet dignity. Each time Hine would persuade him to keep it going for another year. Unlike Florence, who covered thousands of miles a year in her snappy sports cars, the historian used his mainly to tootle up and down Letchworth Hill between home and office. The amusement with which people observed his daily arrival in town was coupled with some admiration for the way he managed to fold his lanky frame to fit inside the tiny vehicle. Like one of those genial eccentrics from an Ealing Studios film, he crouched over the steering wheel with his knees almost touching his chin. To give himself more headroom, he kept the car's sunroof open and each time he spotted a friend a long arm of the Law would appear through the roof to deliver a cheery wave.

Few ever forgot the lifts he gave them. Rhona Garratt, who was articled to Reginald Hartley and later became Assistant Solicitor in the partnership, once recalled a summer's afternoon in the late 1940s when Hine decided it was too hot to work and invited the girls in the office up to Willian Bury 'to take tea.' As none had any transport of their own he persuaded all five to squeeze into his car. What followed was the most frightening journey of their young lives as *Sir Henry*, belching steam from his radiator cap, lurched dangerously through the town and out along the winding lanes to Willian. From her cramped position in a rear seat, beneath the colleague who was sitting on her lap, Rhona spotted a St Christopher medallion on the dashboard. 'Throughout the journey I never took my eyes off it,' she said. 'We were terrified.'

Margaret Barrett, ('Miss Robinson', as she then was) lived on the route that Hine took to the office each morning and, if he spotted her waiting at the bus stop, he would stop to pick her up. Once, as she climbed into the front passenger seat, Margaret noticed a small box and some patches of white powder on the carpet beneath her feet. Her chauffeur apologised for the mess, explaining that he had just returned from scattering the ashes of a deceased client and there had been 'a bit of an accident' when he picked up the box.

He still liked to cycle to work occasionally and on wet days Brenda King ('Miss Royal') never forgot the sight of him pedalling into Hitchin on his *Golden Sunbeam*; steering the machine erratically with one hand and holding a large umbrella aloft with the other. Even more ancient than *Sir Henry*, the bicycle had been bequeathed to him by a farmer, William Wylie of Ashwell. When Hine was drawing up the old man's will Wylie had told him: 'They say you are the worst driver anywhere in the county. As you are bound to kill yourself, and perhaps some of the King's lieges too, I want you to accept a bicycle from me and promise to give up the car.' Hine told him he could not give up driving but later admitted that during World War II, when petrol was scarce, the *Golden Sunbeam* had indeed been worth its weight in gold.

Even in his later years Hine was admired as much by younger women as by those of his own generation. Margaret Payne of Letchworth remembered how his visits brightened the costive atmosphere of the Clerk's department of Hitchin Urban District Council, where she worked as a typist: 'It was an awful fusty place, like something from the Dickensian era. All the girls had to dress soberly in dresses with long sleeves; so when Mr Hine walked in, wearing his loud ginger tweed suit and colourful bow tie the whole room seemed to light up. He was extremely good looking and had a very mischievous sense of humour that annoyed the Clerk to the Council, Mr Passingham. *He* was the exact opposite, terribly old-fashioned and still wearing high wing collars and black ties. It was pretty clear he didn't approve of Mr Hine at all.'

Betty Clarke came to Hitchin in 1947 to join the teaching staff of Old Hale Way School. Asked by her headmistress to set a social project for the older girls, she chose the history of the town and wrote to Hine for advice. He replied immediately and, on learning that she was new to the district, took her on a personal tour of St Mary's Church and the Biggin Almshouses. Their afternoon ended at Hermitage Tea Rooms, a genteel establishment just round the corner from Hine's office and a popular social venue for the town's well-to-do. Elderly ladies whose affairs the lawyer looked after would try hard to obtain a mid-afternoon appointment, in the hope that he would invite them to 'take tea' there once business was done. He frequently obliged, although sometimes the courtesy became more of a chore than a pleasure. He once stormed back into the office to announce: 'I'm afraid I was unable to see with whom I was taking tea today. The woman insisted upon wearing that damned hat and veil throughout.'

This waspish humour can also be found in surviving letters. Replying to a client who had offered to donate a Samuel Lucas oil painting to Hitchin Museum, Hine recalled that it had originally belonged to one of the artist's relatives. 'I used to take state tea with Marianne Lucas once a year and remember the oil painting on her staircase fairly well,' he wrote, 'but it never pleased me very much. In fact, my hostess was so ugly that she seemed to make all her possessions ugly too. So it may look somewhat better now it is out of her house and in yours.' Such stories have survived because of the blessed fact that few people ever threw away a letter signed 'Reginald L. Hine.' Frequently, he would put as much thought into the composition of the shortest letter as he did into the text of his books; so the simplest note of thanks, having brought a flush of pleasure to the recipient, would be carefully tucked away in a bureau drawer. Read today, they reflect that vintage period of English letter writing that has all but disappeared in our 21st-century world of text messages and misspelled e-mails.

A couple who celebrated their Diamond Wedding in 2004 still treasure two letters received from Hine at the time of their war-time wedding, when the young husband was flying on dangerous missions into occupied Europe. Because the bride was under age, her father had objected to the marriage saying that, with the Allies' invasion imminent, he did not want to see his daughter widowed in her first year of married life. When he continued to withhold consent after she had reached her eighteenth birthday, the couple sought Hine's help in obtaining a court order to enable the wedding to go ahead. In the event, the father withdrew his objection and when the couple married at St Mary's Church Hine was a guest. As he had refused to charge a fee for his services, the newlyweds sent him an antique silver candle-snuffer and tray to mark their gratitude. Here is part of his letter of thanks:

It was a kind letter you wrote to me (and rich reward for what
I had been *glad* to do) and your gift is a deep satisfaction and a
lasting delight. I *used* to have a snuffer and tray, for I was long in a
house lit only with candles, and when I was married it was candles
still. I love them and use them. But they were poor in design
and in the end I got rid of them. Now, thanks to your generosity
and discriminating eyes, I have another set of very elegant
workmanship (ornate but not too ornate) and I have placed them,
for my daily pleasure and that of my clients, between the two 1783
silver candlesticks that once belonged to Mr Justice Darling. Some
day you must have office-tea with me by candlelight and see how
well your gift harmonises with its surroundings.

Shortly before Christmas 1944, with peace on the horizon, he
wrote to them again:

In spite of this last week's set-back, I think the end of the war is in
sight; and at this blessed season there is a foretaste of peace in the
waiting-places of the mind. May it come *soon*! Yes: indeed you two
must long to have your own house and habitation, and I shall love
to watch it take on your own character and image, slowly being
enriched with the things that you are collecting. I tease you often
and always shall, but I am sure you two possess a good 'design for
living' and will make something very happy for yourselves and
attractive and enduring for others out of your married life. It is
good of you to confer, in advance, the freedom of your house upon
me, and you may be sure I shall take advantage of it. There will
have to be a *plum tree*, for I am very fond of plum jam for tea.

* * *

Although Florence Hine outlived her husband by more than
thirty years, she could rarely be persuaded to speak about their
relationship. Like most women of her generation she would not
have dreamed of discussing such personal matters with younger
members of her family. Only once, it seems, did she allow her
guard to slip, when she dropped a strong hint to a niece that her

final distancing from Reg had been caused by his close friendship with another woman. Although she named no names it is more than likely that she was referring to a personable Quaker widow who lived on the outskirts of Letchworth Garden City, just across the fields from Willian Bury.

Will and Margaret Harvey had moved to Manor Way in Letchworth in 1934 with their children Mark and Sally. Dr Harvey had been badly injured while serving as a surgeon-lieutenant on a Royal Navy destroyer during the First World War. In 1918, the year that he and Margaret were married, he was awarded the Albert Medal 'for gallantry in saving life at sea.' Only later did his family learn how he had placed his own life in jeopardy to operate on a crewman who was trapped by an arm in the flooded engine room of their sinking ship. Having successfully freed the man by amputating the arm, Harvey collapsed, his lungs irreparably damaged by the fumes he had inhaled while performing the improvised operation.

Unable to continue with his peacetime career in adult education this committed and gentle Quaker turned to writing. Probably his best-loved book was *We Were Seven*, a memoir based on his Quaker childhood in Yorkshire. However, it was his horror stories that earned him most critical acclaim. Among these was *The Beast with Five Fingers* (1928), a rather comical tale about a disembodied hand that scuttles about a Sussex mansion. The family had always considered this story to be far from his best, so they must have been surprised and perhaps a little embarrassed when, in 1946, it was bought by Warner Brothers, re-located to an Italian castle and turned into a Hollywood horror film starring Peter Lorre.

Will Harvey died in 1937 at the age of fifty-two. His widow Margaret (1898-1991) was a striking and widely gifted woman. As a Quaker she had been educated at the Society of Friends' Mount School in York. She had planned to read history at Oxford but war and the teenage romance with her second cousin Will led to this plan being abandoned in favour of an early marriage. Although her husband's frailty and continuing bouts of illness placed additional burdens on her domestic life, Margaret still found time to pursue her special talent for drawing and painting. From her schooldays until she was in her eighties, her pencils, sketchbooks, paintbrushes and canvases went everywhere with her. She later became a governor of the St Alban's School of Art, where there is now a Margaret Harvey Gallery in her memory. With widowhood, Margaret plunged herself into public work. In 1938 she was elected a Labour member of Letchworth Urban District Council and was the first woman to become chairman. She was also a Justice of the Peace and served on Hertfordshire Education Committee for many years.

Hine had been solicitor and friend to the Harveys since their arrival at Letchworth from Surrey in 1934. It was immediately after Will's death that the welfare and future security of Margaret and her children became a matter of acute personal concern for him. Having seen her safely through all the legal problems and secured a war widow's pension for her, he became a constant caller. To Sally and her brother he was a figure of great reassurance and security. 'I have very vivid recollections of his quite unannounced visits,' Sally wrote. 'He always seemed so much at home with us all and provided a wonderful boost to our morale.'

Throughout the war years, when the children were completing their education at St Christopher School in Letchworth, Hine wrote them numerous affectionate letters of encouragement and support, referring to himself as 'your friend and erstwhile appointed guardian.' One, written on Christmas Day 1941 to thank Sally for a present, contains a revealing aside: 'Tell that nice mother of yours (whose card stands first and foremost on my mantel-piece) that if she has any of that plum jam left I'll come round these hols to gorge and gossip.' Apart from re-affirming his passion for plum jam, there is more than a hint of his fondness for Sally's mother as well. Three years later, on Christmas Day 1944, he gave Margaret a pre-publication copy of *Confessions of An Un-Common Attorney*. The rather coy inscription inside reads: 'I don't mind confessing to *you* for, though you are a magistrate for the county of Hertford, you are also my very good friend and would always give me the benefit of the doubt, or put me on probation for the rest of my unnatural life.'

Having been widowed at the age of thirty-eight, Margaret Harvey was not short of male admirers and her teenage children would frequently tease their mother about what were collectively known as her 'nice little men' who came calling. According to her daughter, she seemed oblivious of their attention. 'My mother was colourful, eloquent, great fun and with her own special flair and style. I don't think she was quite aware of the effect she had on people. Perhaps she simply did not know how to handle admiration.' However, both Sally and Mark soon realised that their mother's friendship with Hine held something very special. They began to detect an undercurrent of suppressed excitement, a 'buzz' of anticipation, when it was known that Mr Hine would be coming to tea:

> 'My brother and I did not talk about this together but I think we both sensed that something important, complex and private had developed between them and in this we had no part. There was a tension and a shared zest; a strong understanding between them that was something quite apart from the many interests they had in common. They were two remarkable and complex people who, in their different ways, were both on the local public stage. Although there was nothing mysterious or secret in their friendship, I feel there was much that remained private to them.'

This is not to suggest that an *affaire* took place. For those were days when responsible men and women who found themselves in a deepening relationship that threatened a conflict of loyalties would 'do the right thing' and remain apart physically. As Margaret Harvey's daughter put it: 'In these matters, both would have had strict unspoken codes in which loyalty and honour would have ruled ... Nevertheless, I know that Mr Hine loved our family and expressed this freely to my brother and me in his letters and gifts. I can only remind myself how lucky we were to have, for ten of our young years, his lively friendship and encouragement while guessing nothing of his life-long shadows.'

In fact, one of those shadows did follow Hine into the Harvey household. The family became puzzled by the fact that, although he visited them frequently and greatly enjoyed their company there was never a reciprocal invitation to take tea at Willian Bury, so close by.

Sally remembered how the historian would dismiss abruptly any mention of his own family: 'Of course, we knew of his wife Florence and daughter Felicity but he refused to speak of them. I remember my mother was quite shocked at his lack of enthusiasm when we congratulated him on the birth of his first grandson. For her it seemed such a natural reason for celebration but he just brushed it aside.'

This behaviour is strangely reminiscent of the plot of one of Alan Ayckbourn's best and saddest plays. Written in 1985, *Woman in Mind* tells of a vicar's wife who is trapped in an unhappy marriage and invents a dream family to provide the affection and understanding that is totally lacking in her own. Gradually she begins to lose control over these idealised people until she finds herself in a fantasy world involving both real and imaginary families. In the years that followed Will Harvey's death, the Hine family unit had begun to disintegrate further. After Felicity's wedding in 1938 Reg and Florence lived ever more separate lives, his far lonelier than hers. Suddenly, as guide and counsellor to Margaret and her children, Hine had found his own 'dream family.' He was a surrogate father to two bright and appreciative youngsters whose mother not only shared his love of literature and the arts but also showed him the affection, companionship and understanding that was no longer evident at home.

Thus, when he entered her world to 'gorge and gossip' over tea, bread-and-butter and plum jam, he resented any intrusive mention of his own, less happy domestic life. We know from other sources that he was immensely proud of the arrival of his first grandson but even that event was allowed no place in the home of his second family. That Margaret Harvey had something more than a passing affection for Reginald Hine there can be no doubt. Many wept when they learned of the terrible way he chose to end his life. 'My mother was a very strong woman,' said her daughter. 'But when she learned of the tragedy she was absolutely distraught.'

[10]
'Tall Men are Like Poplar Trees'

T HE TELEPHONE MESSAGE was urgent and delivered just in
time. Hine jumped up from his desk, hurried across to the
door of his office and locked it. Ten seconds later heavy footsteps
in the corridor stopped outside and the doorknob turned. The
unwanted caller, realising he had been foiled, let fly a torrent of
verbal abuse and started thumping on the door with his fists. Hine,
fearing for his safety, grabbed the Victorian police truncheon
that hung on the wall and waited nervously for the door to burst
open. Fortunately for him it stood firm. In the meantime Dulcie
Stapleton, who ran Hartley & Hine's front office, had foreseen
trouble and telephoned the Police Station. Within a couple of
minutes two of its larger occupants had hurried across the street
to 109 Bancroft and after a short tussle the angry client was
persuaded to leave.

The incident left a lasting impression on Audrey Farr who,
in 1944, had just joined the law firm as a secretary: 'The man
was going through a divorce,' she recalled. 'Five weeks earlier he
had asked Mr Hine to represent him and because he had done
absolutely nothing about it, the man's patience had snapped. He
stormed into the office in a furious rage. When Dulcie asked him
if he could wait while she made inquiries he shouted that he'd had
enough of waiting and was going up to sort Hine out there and
then. There was just time to pick up the phone and warn Mr Hine
to lock his door. It was quite frightening really because the client
was a very big man and we had no doubt that he was planning
to use his fists on him. The noise he was making could be heard
out in the street and by the time the police arrived a small crowd
had gathered.'

Like many local girls of the Forties and Fifties Audrey Mayes,
as she then was, had spent two years learning shorthand and
typing at Mullarkey's Commercial College in Old Park Road
before being taken on by the law firm for a modest weekly wage

of 7s 6d (£32 when adjusted to the average earnings of today).

It was clear to even this newest member of staff that Reggie Hine was no longer interested in the job to which (as he frequently reminded everyone) it had *not* pleased God to call him.

In fact, the angry divorcee was one of several frustrated clients who had been driven to protest about the lawyer's increasingly lackadaisical approach to dealing with their problems. As a rule, it was Dulcie Stapleton who bore the brunt of these complaints. Quite frequently she would find herself involved in 'frantic last-minute scrambles' before marching into her employer's office and plonking the relevant file down in front of him with the instruction: 'Mr Hine. This has to be done … TODAY.'

Whenever he was dictating details of a will or a conveyance to his new secretary Hine needed only the slightest excuse to break off and talk about something closer to his heart. Audrey lost count of the number of times she had to put down her pencil and sit gazing at the gold-framed Canaletto painting on the wall while Hine enthused about it. At other times he would break off and launch into a ten-minute lecture about the derivation of a word he had just used. 'He was,' she said, 'an absolute dreamer who had lost all interest in his work as a solicitor.' A fact confirmed by her employer himself one afternoon when he suddenly stopped in mid-sentence, leaned back in his chair with a heavy sigh and said: 'You know Miss Mayes, I don't really want to do this work any more. I just want to be able to write my books. That's all. Just to be left alone to read and to write.'

Word among the local magistrates was that the historian could never bring himself to defend people whom he knew to be guilty. In the privacy of his office he would ask clients whether or not they had committed the crime with which they were charged. If they confessed, but still wished to plead 'Not Guilty,' Hine would say 'I think it would be far safer if your case was handled by my partner,' and pass them over to Reginald Hartley. It was not long before their worships got wind of this idiosyncrasy and found themselves having to tread with more care than usual when deciding if the various clients of Mr Hartley and Mr Hine were innocent or guilty.

As legal work became more irksome so the historian's ways of avoiding it became more eccentric. A secretary bringing clients up to his office would knock, open the door and find nobody there, even though they had just spoken on the office intercom. After checking in all the likely places, the girl would have to show out the bemused visitors with the promise that she would contact them as soon as Mr Hine had been found. A few minutes later the missing solicitor would appear and sheepishly confess that, at the last minute, he had suffered an anxiety attack and been unable to face them. When the secretary opened the door he had been down on his hands and knees, hiding behind the desk.

This behaviour was partially explained at Hine's inquest in 1949, when Dr Howard Dumere revealed that he had been treating his patient for threatened nervous breakdowns for thirteen years. That is to say, since 1936 when the lawyer had to give up his cosy sinecure with Hawkins & Co. and, for the first time in his life, stand on his own two feet. With the advantage of hindsight it is clear that he should have taken his doctor's advice and stopped practising while his health and his reputation were still intact. By the end of the war Hine was in his early sixties; a perfectly respectable age at which to make a dignified exit. Yet, in March 1945, he had ignored the ideal retirement opportunity when the triumphant publication of *Confessions of an Un-common Attorney* would have enabled him to bow out of the profession in a blaze of glory. The cruel irony is that, if he *had* taken that option, he would not have found himself in the situation that four years later drove him to suicide.

This determination to hang on in a profession that he no longer enjoyed becomes even harder to comprehend when *Confessions* itself contains a clear admission that the author was already aware of his delicate mental state and was having great difficulty in coping with the pressures of law work. The most revealing passage centres on the choice of quotation from a Hertfordshire lawyer of Elizabethan times, the philosopher and statesman Francis Bacon, Viscount St Albans (1561-1626):

Lanky and loose-limbed solicitors are always the first to fall, for there is stinging truth in what the little man Francis Bacon said: 'Tall men are like poplar trees, which do die from the top.' . . . When I resorted to the doctors, they spoke learnedly of alopecia and neurasthenia but could do nothing for either. If I would be so unwise as to live beyond my income of vital energy I must expect to be in difficulties. Clearly the strain of leading a double life, the accumulation of office worries, and the burden of clients' woes had worn me down. It is in nervous disorders, above all, that a man should be his own physician, for each of us has his own familiar fiend and should know best how to wrestle with him . . .

When the doctors had the honesty to confess they could not help me, I saw that I must work out my own salvation. Not by indifference nor by callousness but of hard necessity I began to grow a tough hide for this exasperating world. Something delicate and sensitive in one has to die, but it is the only way. People who don't live are wonderfully preserved. But those who are obliged to live are in continual danger. Needs must that offences come, and in the profession of the law they are coming every day. Many a letter in the morning post will be a minor shock. And there are major shocks. Questions of conscience, legal and personal, arise and these are the most injurious of all. I once heard a neurologist say that one hour's conflict of mind or indecision on a point of conscience can work more havoc on the nervous system than a year of drinking and debauch.'

The final lines reveal Hine's most vulnerable weakness. As he grew older, and the neuroses suffered since his youth became more acute, he seems to have lost the lawyer's essential ability to detach himself emotionally from the problems of those who came to him for advice. Opening the morning post had become a lonely and sometimes distressing job. No longer did it take place over coffee, toast and marmalade in the reassuring presence of Onslow Times, whose wisdom had always guided him safely through the day's decisions. Having to cope on his own left Hine fraught by daily pressures and anxieties that would frequently cause him to flee his office and disappear on long walks to try to clear his head.

This growing disillusion with his profession is reflected also in the entry that he submitted for the 1948 edition of *Who's Who*. It is all about 'Hine the Historian.' Apart from a passing reference to the fact that he was also a solicitor, there are no details whatever of his career in the law.

> **HINE, Reginald Leslie**, F.S.A., F.R.Hist.S; historian and
> solicitor; b.25 Sept, 1883; *s.* of Neville Joseph and Eliza Hine,
> Newnham Hall, Herts; *m* 1912, Florence Lee Pyman; one *d.*
> Educ: privately and The Leys School, Cambridge. *Publications:*
> Anima Celtica, 1910; Dreams and the Way of Dreams, 1913; The
> Cream of Curiosity, 1920; The History of Hitchin (2 vols), 1927-29;
> Hitchin Worthies, 1932; Natural History of the Hitchin Region,
> 1934; Confessions of an Un-Common Attorney (3rd ed.) 1947.
> *Recreation:* exploring every nook and cranny of Hertfordshire.
> *Address:* Willian Bury, Willian, Hertfordshire. *T.A:* Hine, Hitchin.
> *T.:* Letchworth 532. *Club:* The Tomorrow.

Although writing *Confessions* probably served as an antidote to the combined stresses of work and the war years, the book's very success brought new pressures to bear. Having been accorded international recognition by his readers, he found them anxious to know when his next volume would be in the shops. Most eagerly awaited were a companion to *Hitchin Worthies* and his *History of Hertfordshire*, the research material for which already filled sixty large box files. However, continuing pressure from his obligations to Hartley & Hine caused the historian to slip further and further behind with the heavy writing schedule he had given himself.

By the end of 1946 those asking about progress with the county history usually received the same self-deprecating reply: 'It crawls on as slowly as a snail, nay worse, as slow as a solicitor.' To one reader from Bishops Stortford, Hine's curt response suggests he was becoming rattled by the persistent inquiries: 'For goodness sake be patient about my *History of Hertfordshire*. I have your name and address and shall hope to send you a prospectus some day.' By this time he was beginning to have doubts that the history would ever be completed. He hinted as much during his Jubilee speech to East Herts Archaeological Society in September 1948: 'Often,

of a Saturday afternoon, and having escaped from the Law, I sit in
the British Museum working on a History of Hertfordshire that
I may never finish …'

Conversely that same speech, made only months before his
death, revealed that Hine had lost none of his skill as an orator.
Delivered to a packed Council Chamber at Hertford's County
Hall, it proved to be a *tour-de-force*, attracting such epithets as
'masterly' and 'brilliant.' Although it is best remembered now
for his confession about the 'Roman Urn' incident, the address
also provided a detailed record of the vast amount of historical
research achieved during the society's first fifty years. Typically,
the duller facts were interspersed with entertaining anecdotes, not
least about those weekend 'excursions' that are recalled in the first
chapter of this book:

> It can have been no edifying sight to watch us swarming here,
> there, and everywhere about some hallowed building before the
> paper was delivered. Each hobbyist would follow his own bent.
> If Squires' F.R.C.O. brother were lost to view we knew where to
> find him – exploring the bowels, the innermost recesses of the
> organ. H. C. Andrews might be seen perched on the top of a
> pew or mounting a windowsill in search of a mason's mark. Some
> members would be down upon hands and knees deciphering
> brasses …
>
> If you missed William Graveson, he could be discovered
> botanizing upon some ill-kept, overgrown grave, whilst Gerish,
> with scrubbing brush and notebook in hand, would be scouring the
> stones and copying the epitaphs. My own preference was to occupy
> the scant interval of time taking rubbings of medieval graffiti, or
> I would hunt for the headstone and iron ring leading to the vault
> of some Hertfordshire family in which I was interested, so that I
> could return some day, obtain help to lift the stone, and ghoulishly
> descend. I am no morbid moraliser amongst the tombs, but I like
> to follow those of whom I happen to be writing as far as one can
> go this side of eternity. And strange things are to be seen down
> amongst dead men in their vaults.

This was Hine's last major speech. Fortunately for the archaeological society and for us it is preserved word for word among the bound copies of their magazine *Transactions*, which are now held by the Local Studies Archive in the very building where the speech was delivered.

One other lecture preserved in its entirety is, of course, *'A Walk Up Tilehouse Street.'* News of its discovery and this author's re-creation of it at the Hitchin Festival in 2001 stirred the memories of a few people who had heard the original. Apparently it was delivered one December evening in 1941 in a blacked-out town hall, where Hine's entertaining mixture of history and gossip offered a welcome distraction from the horrors of the London Blitz:

> Let us halt for a moment by the corner house, No 19, where once Mrs Smallwood lived. She was the daughter of Professor Lax of St Ippolyts and her husband was killed in a riot in Monte Video. By all accounts, she must have been a rather eccentric lady for, as she opened the door to you on a winter's day, she would often have a flannel petticoat swathed about her head. One afternoon she was entertaining a well-known townsman to tea, a man with an artificial leg which, for comfort's sake, he used to unscrew and place beside his chair. Halfway through tea there came a knock at the door and Mrs Smallwood, not wishing to be discovered with a member of the opposite sex, bundled him into a cupboard and then opened the front door. Alas, the wooden leg had been forgotten. The visitor saw and smiled. By the next afternoon, the whole of Hitchin knew.

Despite his wide experience as a public speaker Hine never liked to extemporise. Every talk he gave involved several hours of preparation, writing page after page of notes in a spidery longhand that none but he could read. All marked up with an elaborate system of numbers and 'pointers' to help him achieve dramatic emphasis. The size of the audience was not important to him. A handful of young people in a chapel schoolroom or a dozen elderly ladies clustered around a coke stove in a village hall would be treated to a talk over which he had taken as much care had he been preparing a lecture for the Royal Historical Society. The more genteel souls among his listeners would on occasions find themselves shocked (or secretly thrilled) by daring tales of the gypsies and poachers he had befriended while exploring the nooks and crannies of his county.

Inevitably, Hine's high profile brought him numerous invitations to hold honorary posts with a variety of organisations across the county. When the Bancroft Players Amateur Dramatic Society was founded in Hitchin in 1945 he became their Vice-President. Members from those early days recalled his habit of arriving slightly late for performances; a discourtesy that left the company on tenterhooks wondering whether they should delay 'Curtain Up' so that Mr Hine would not miss the opening. For the sake of the rest of the audience they usually went ahead, only to be upstaged (or in this case *down* staged) by the unmistakable silhouette of their tall Vice-President, with his special cushion under his arm, being guided by torchlight to his front row seat. Some frustrated organisers were convinced that these habitually late arrivals were not so much accidental as carefully timed to ensure that his entrance made the maximum impact. A fellow historian, W. Branch Johnson of Welwyn, was sure it was all part of the image Hine wanted to create:

> With most local historians their works are of their lives a
> thing apart. But the personality of Hine was, so to speak, his
> whole existence. Everything he wrote, everything he did was a
> flamboyant manifestation of it. His talk (he kept his black words
> to himself) was invariably refreshing – bubbling, humorous, laced
> with picturesque stories and delicately attuned to his immediate
> company. When he entered a meeting or a concert hall, often
> with an 18th-century quarto volume under his arm, a faint stir ran
> through the audience. He would have failed in his mission if he
> had not dramatised himself as a Hitchin Worthy.

This 'Worthy' status was further enhanced in December 1945 when Hine was invited to give a radio talk about his town. The twelve-minute broadcast featured on *From All Over Britain*, a weekly magazine programme transmitted at home and abroad by the B.B.C. Overseas Service. Although the Corporation's archive department still holds a copy of the original script, it did not consider the recording to be worth keeping. Fortunately, the historian had other ideas and managed to charm his producer, Mrs M.J. Davy, into having an additional copy cut especially for him. During sixty years of casual storage in family cupboards, this sole surviving recording of Hine's voice has lost much of its original quality; some sections having disappeared altogether. However, with the help of computer technology, it has been possible to salvage a seven-minute version that is now preserved for posterity on compact disc.

Listening to it one understands why Hine became known as 'The last of the Edwardians.' His voice has a quaint, precise ring about it, reminiscent of a 1930s broadcast by Prime Minister Neville Chamberlain. There are also one or two examples of the curious pronunciations that he liked to affect in everyday life and which some of his friends found rather tedious. Guy Salusbury-Hughes, a friend and fellow cricketer, who lived at Offley, near Hitchin, was one. Although his family name has been spelt with a 'U' for centuries, it is pronounced in exactly the same way as the cathedral city in Wiltshire. For some reason (whether it was mischief or pure affectation is hard to guess) Hine always made a great point of stressing the 'U.' Eventually Salusbury-Hughes lost patience and penned the following piece of doggerel which Hine found in his mail one morning:

> My Dear Mr Hine,
> I wish you'd refrain
> From mispronouncing
> Our family name.
> Though I don't as a rule
> Say 'Boo!' to a goose
> It is quite incorrect
> To call me 'Saloose' (bury).
> All of which

I hope you'll excuse
From your very good friend
Guy Salusbury-Hughes.

To the majority of people in post war Hertfordshire the public image of Reginald Hine changed very little. He was, perhaps, a little frailer and his tall figure had become somewhat stooped. Yet he still effused confidence in his determination to perpetuate that image of a Hitchin Worthy; carrying his walking stick with a swing as he strode down the High Street in his tweed suit, bow tie and spats, distributing greetings to all and sundry. If it was mid-morning he was more than likely heading for his first floor window seat at Nott's Coffee House, where he had an unbreakable daily assignation with some of his old chums; the artist Gerard Ceunis, Ernest Hodson, editor of the *Hertfordshire Express* and the bookseller Basil Donne-Smith.

At one such gathering midway through 1948 his friends began to sense that Hine was deeply preoccupied with a problem. Although they never sought to discover what it was, they could tell that it was something more serious than the customary bouts of anxiety and depression with which they were all too familiar. The plain fact was that 'the tough hide' that Hine had grown to cope with the pressures of life had landed him in trouble. In his increasing contempt for the profession that was interfering with his work as an historian, he was not averse to flouting its rules. Now, some of his fellow lawyers had finally run out of patience and were about to take him to task for it.

[11]
'A Rascally Attorney'

THE LAW SOCIETY, which represents and regulates solicitors in England and Wales, has always taken a strong line against members who indulge in unapproved forms of self-promotion. When its Rules of Practice were updated in 1936, the new Rule One declared:

> A solicitor shall not directly or indirectly apply for or seek instructions for professional business or do or permit in the carrying on of his practice any act or thing which can reasonably be regarded as touting or advertising or as calculated to attract business unfairly.

The rule lasted in that form until 1971 when it was again amended to take account of the greater freedoms accorded to the profession in this field. Today, there is a Solicitors' Disciplinary Tribunal, established by Act of Parliament and constitutionally independent of the Law Society. Although the Society has long had power to impose fines and even to bar serious offenders from continuing in practice, solicitors are encouraged whenever possible to try to resolve disciplinary matters locally. This is what happened when Reginald Hine first blotted his lawyer's copybook in the late 1930s.

A year or two after setting up in partnership with Reginald Hartley, he found himself facing allegations that he had tried to poach the clients of other local solicitors by the aforesaid 'touting or advertising.' He was accused of writing letters to those individuals involved in legal transactions with his own clients suggesting that he could save them money by acting for both sides at the same time. In the 1930s, legal practice in the little market town was still being run on the lines of a rather exclusive private club. The senior members of the coterie, having met to discuss Hine's indiscretions, decided to deliver a stern warning.

A tersely worded letter was sent calling upon him to desist from touting for business in this way and cautioning him that, if he did not, he could be reported to the Law Society. The letter was sent as a 'Round Robin,' the signatures forming a circle to emphasise that the town's solicitors were acting as a unanimous group with no single leader.

One would have thought that the serious implications behind this letter would have sounded sufficient alarm bells to put any errant lawyer back onto the straight and narrow for the rest of his career. Not so with Hine. Some ten years later, in August 1948, he was again reported for touting and again did not contest the allegations. On this occasion he was told that, to avoid being reported to the Law Society, he would have to make a written undertaking not to continue the malpractice. So, on August 31st, Hitchin's uncommon attorney signed a confession that does not feature in his book:

> I, Reginald Leslie Hine agree that I have on a number of occasions when acting for one party to a transaction, written letters to the other which amount to touting and advertising within the meaning of Rule 1 of the Solicitors' Practice Rules 1936. In such a letter written personally to _____on 13th July 1948 the suggestion was made that it might save expense if Reginald Leslie Hine acted for both parties. I hereby undertake that no further letters or other advances of this nature will in future be made.
> *Signed*: Reginald L. Hine
> *Witness*: W. O. Times, Hitchin, Herts, solicitor.

By making Hine sign this undertaking, the elders of Hitchin's legal fraternity had managed to forestall a fairly sensational local scandal. So discreetly was the affair handled that, for half a century and despite the dramatic circumstances surrounding his death, only a handful of lawyers ever knew just how much trouble Hine had been in. Even his family was unaware until the relevant documents were uncovered during the research for this book.

* * *

At the time that he gave the undertaking, the historian was well on his way to completing another volume. Having realised that his *History of Hertfordshire* was not going to get off the ground he decided to divert some of the unused fruits of his research into a different project. Over the years he had assembled a considerable amount of material relating to the romantic essayist Charles Lamb (1775-1834). *Elia* (to use Lamb's pen name) was a Londoner but had spent much of his childhood consorting with 'cousins sprinkled all over Hertfordshire.' As a result the county features in much of his writing. Hine was a passionate devotee of Lamb's work and when a group of Elian enthusiasts founded the Charles Lamb Society in 1935 he was one of the first to join.

At the society's autumn gathering in Bloomsbury in 1947, the historian delivered a lecture about Lamb's Hertfordshire connections. The plaudits that followed convinced him that his story would do well in print and within a few weeks he had persuaded J.M. Dent & Son to publish what was intended to be a slim volume based upon his lecture. However, Hine being Hine, *Charles Lamb & His Hertfordshire* grew like Topsy into a solid volume of some four hundred pages. As he delved deeper into Lamb's life, the historian found himself developing a strong spiritual bond with his subject. It was this bond that became his refuge during the last troubled days of his life.

Despite being in his mid-sixties and in far from good health, Hine insisted on continuing with the punishing work schedule that he had adopted twenty years earlier. Practising law by day and writing at night; retiring exhausted at midnight to sleep fitfully for a few hours before rising at 3.30 a.m. to return to his manuscript. For most of the time he and his wife only ever met at breakfast and dinner. Florence was still working hard for local good causes, notably the Red Cross and the Girl Guide movement. Since purchasing Willian Bury her interests had become centred less on Hitchin and more on the Garden City where she joined a number of the popular intellectual groups that had become a feature of the community. She would have liked to spend more time with Felicity and the grandchildren but they were now abroad for much of the year.

After leaving the R.A.F., Bill McEwen returned to his job with the Sudan Political Service in Khartoum. His family joined him later, travelling to North Africa by cargo boat. It was an eventful voyage for Felicity during which her second-born Michael almost perished. One evening, the energetic three-year-old was spotted squeezing out of the cabin porthole. Fortunately he became stuck and his mother just managed to grab him by the seat of his pants. It was Michael's second narrow escape; during the war, when a bomb fell on the house next door to where the family was living, he had been blown out of his cot by the blast. The oldest of the brothers, Andrew, remembers their few years in Sudan as extremely happy and packed with adventure:

'We had a lovely house in the centre of Khartoum and my father kept a sailing boat on the Nile. He would tow us behind it, letting us hang onto a rope that trailed from the stern. Of course, we had to take constant precautions about crocodiles. Even quite close to the capital we could see them lying in rows along the river bank pretending to be asleep, when in fact they were waiting for prey to take a fatal incautious step too close. My parents told me that, before the war, they used to go swimming at a place called Gordon's Tree. As the river there was infested with large and very hungry crocodiles, one person was always posted on shore with a powerful rifle. On one occasion when my grandmother was standing guard a crocodile showed serious intentions of having my parents for lunch. She killed the beast with a single well-aimed bullet. I suppose all this sounds very dramatic in the safety conscious 21st Century but it was in no way remarkable in Sudan at that time.'

Without the lively presence of the McEwen family, the atmosphere at Willian Bury at times resembled that of a mausoleum. Florence was now sharing her home with not one but two solitary men. Her brother Geoffrey Pyman had moved in and was occupying what was euphemistically described as 'a bachelor pad' in one corner of the big house. Geoffrey had been the only other member of the Pyman family to remain in Hertfordshire after his mother and brothers returned to London in 1906. Good-looking and athletic he was a popular figure in the county. Of the three Pyman brothers who went to war in 1914 he had been the only one to survive. He reached the rank of Lieutenant Colonel and returned a much-decorated hero, having been awarded both the Military Cross and a Distinguished Service Order 'for conspicuous ability and devotion to duty' during the fighting around Ypres and at the Battle of the Piave. For his part in this last action he also received the *Croce della Guerra* from the Italian government.

As a director of the Pyman Brothers' ship-broking firm in Bishopsgate, Geoffrey divided his time between the City and North Hertfordshire, where he had an active and enjoyable social life. He was an outstanding golfer and tennis player and his fine singing voice gained him several leading roles in the Gilbert and Sullivan productions of Hitchin Thespians operatic society. In 1922 he married his first cousin Blanche Gray Pyman and they had one child, Paul, born in 1929. For several years, the family lived at Norman's Farm, quite close to Willian Bury. One January morning in the mid-1930s Geoffrey's life was devastated when his wife walked out of the house with their small son and did not return. It was a shock from which he never fully recovered, not least because Blanche gave no reason why she had left him. Their brother-in-law relished telling a rather cruel story of how, when asked what she would like for Christmas that year, Blanche told her husband that she had never had a decent set of travelling cases. Geoffrey duly bought her some and barely a fortnight later she filled them with her belongings and departed.

It was following this domestic calamity that the trustees of the Pyman estate (of which Geoffrey was one) agreed that he could live in his sister's house. Hine had no say in this matter, nor it seems in any other relating to Willian Bury. When the house and grounds were transferred to Florence in 1941 following her father's death she immediately created a new trust naming herself and Felicity as trustees together with her accountant John Knowles of Letchworth and Hine's partner Reginald Hartley. Her husband's status in the household may be gauged from an observation made by a friend who, as a young man new to the district, was once invited for lunch: 'There were just the three of us. Mrs Hine was sitting like a matriarch at the head of the table, very forbidding and unbending. I felt quite intimidated by her and I think Reginald did too. It did not seem to me that he was master in his own house.'

In 1947, following one of the coldest and most unpleasant British winters on record, Florence resolved that the next one would be spent in warmer climes. That autumn she left her husband to work on his book while she joined Bill, Felicity and their children in Sudan. The visit was part of a longer journey that took the family almost the length of Africa to spend Christmas with Bill McEwen's parents, who were by this time retired and living near Cape Town. The trip involved several separate journeys by land, sea and air, and is remembered by the three grandsons as one of the great adventures of their young lives. It got off to a dramatic start when the Nile paddle steamer taking them from Khartoum to Uganda ran aground and had to be hauled off a sandbank by hordes of Nuban natives in dug-out canoes. On that same holiday Andrew fell ill with malaria. Following an anxious Christmas it was decided that, instead of returning to Khartoum, the boy should sail back with his grandmother to recuperate in England.

During the twenty-three years that she lived at Willian Bury, Florence employed a daily staff of three or four villagers to look after the house and grounds. On her return to England with Andrew she decided that another pair of hands was needed and in the Spring of 1948 there began a search for a professional nanny to look after her grandsons when they were in this country. With the help of an agency she and Felicity were eventually put in touch with Stella White (later Mrs Stella Edwards) a pretty Cornish lass in her early twenties who quickly won the hearts of the entire family. So much so that Florence invited her to stay on as a permanent companion. Stella remained with the family for more than three years, until her marriage, and did much to help Florence through the crisis of her husband's death.

* * *

Despite the damage sustained to his legal reputation, Hine the historian sailed on unperturbed through the autumn of 1948. On September 15th, a fortnight after signing the 'Touting or Advertising' undertaking, he was at County Hall being feted by the great and the good of Hertfordshire for his 'brilliant address of wit and wisdom' at the Golden Jubilee of East Herts Archaeological Society. On October 11th (as he describes in entertaining detail in *Charles Lamb and His Hertfordshire*) he made one of the most expensive antiquarian purchases of his life when he bid successfully for one of Lamb's handwritten commonplace-books when it came up for auction at Sotheby's. He had not dared to attend the event, leaving it to a literary agent to bid for him:

> Meanwhile, as a common or un-common attorney, I was sitting or rather writhing in agony at my office, giving heedless and reckless advice to most unfortunate clients. Every time the phone rang, my temperature rose. But at last I shouted *'This is terrific'* to a timid, ineffectual, and now suddenly startled little man who had been deserted by his wife. And soon, soon, I was being joined together in idolatry or bibliolatry - till death do us part - with a lovely and bewitching companion that I keep, with pride of place, on my study table by day and under my pillow by night.

When unable to enjoy the company and adulation of fellow historians Hine was beginning to feel less sure of his status among the more down-to-earth members of the community. This fear revealed itself one Monday lunchtime at the Hermitage Halls in Hitchin, when he was guest speaker at the weekly meeting of the Rotary Club. As members walked from the bar to their tables he suddenly gripped the arm of the friend who was acting as his host and whispered urgently: 'Please, come and sit near me. These people don't like me, you know. I need your support.'

The fear was justified to some extent. For by this time there was a ripple of resentment among some of Hitchin's 'influential' citizens that Hine's enduring popularity as an historian and public speaker was gaining him more recognition and respect than those who were making the real contribution to the town's post-war recovery. This hostility was strengthened by the fact that, apart from his occasional work on the Council's Library & Museum Committee, Hine was not really a 'team man.' By his own admission he did not have the patience for the essential grind of committee work and for this reason had refused to stand for election to the local council.

Basil Donne-Smith had noticed the 'touch of the loner' about him. In his preface to the 1972 reprint of *The History of Hitchin* he writes of its author: 'For all his very real affection and thought for his host of acquaintances . . . he was never really at home in the easy camaraderie of Rotary or the Conservative Club.' Donne-Smith's memoir contains the most perceptive surviving description of the historian in his later years and ventures to touch on the reasons for Hine's fragile state of mind and eccentric behaviour:

> One of his many functions, it appeared, was to act as a herald
> of spring. The seasons in our variable climate rarely develop the
> logical sequence of seasons overseas. There is, in early summer,
> an everlasting problem of habiliment. But as soon as R.L.H. had
> donned his gay green suit then we all knew, without doubt, that
> spring had truly arrived. It was a very exceptional season indeed
> in which muffler or even mackintosh were called upon to veil the
> happy sight of Reginald in all his greenery striding down the High
> Street saluting his many friends . . .
>
> For some, it is true, there was more than a hint of theatricality
> in all this. Maybe the laughter was a shade too hearty, the flash of
> the eye too bright. As with the flare in the nostril of a fairground
> horse there was often a feeling of pageantry about him. Indeed one
> could easily feel sometimes when in his company that we were in
> some kind of Watteau-esque *Fête Champêtre* in a crowd of figures
> masquerading in a sort of dreamland charade, divorced from time
> and place. Now there was nothing charlatan about this, nothing
> either pretentious or insincere. There is in all of us some element of
> the changeling, an alternation between fantasy and reality, though
> for most of us the former (at any rate in our adult years) remains
> well hidden under a veneer of conventional behaviour.

A less obedient, a more obtrusive imagination, however, is what makes a good historian, for it enables a man to recognise the value of Myth in the true sense of that much-abused word, and so become much more than a mere recorder of the minutiae of events … All concerned writers are to some extent schizophrenic: it is their torment that constitutes some of the greatest treasures of literature. Nevertheless the stresses thereby created while they may be good for Art are undeniably bad for the maintenance of that even tenor which is the recipe for longevity.

The aside that 'all concerned writers are to some extent schizophrenic' suggests Donne-Smith may have formed a view that Hine's behaviour was caused by a schizoid personality. This is unlikely to have been the case. A consultant psychiatrist who studied the evidence presented in this book believed it more likely that the young Hine had cyclothymia. This disorder consists of a persistent instability of mood that swings between periods of mild depression and mild elation. The depressive mood may have been influenced by the trauma of his mother's death when he was eight years old and later by the rigours of life at boarding school. Such conditions may grow more serious with age, eventually developing into manic-depression, or what is now known as bipolar disorder, when the periods of elation and depression become more pronounced. Thus we had Hine the headstrong extrovert 'his laughter a shade too hearty, the flash of the eye too bright' and Hine the anxious and insecure human being whose private anxieties and periods of depression would one day reach a point at which they became unbearable.

Although the historian wrote with great honesty about his periods of mental turmoil not many readers appreciated just how serious and prolonged they were. Those critics irritated by his public flamboyance might have adopted a more charitable outlook had they known also of the downside of his life. The overbearing and unloving wife, the many lonely nights, the hideous nightmare images and the long pre-dawn hours spent sitting in candlelight with pen, ink and paper, seeking inspiration that was becoming harder to find with every day that passed.

To this sometimes bleak situation at Willian Bury must be added the fact that Hine never really recovered from having to leave Hawkins & Co. in 1936. Following the departure of his mentor Onslow Times he probably believed his reputation as an historian would guarantee him a position with the law firm for the remainder of his career. So to receive what was tantamount to a redundancy notice at the age of fifty-two must have dealt a severe blow to his delicate ego.

Those who knew and respected Hine believe that, while fully capable of mischief and the cutting remark, he was not a malicious or spiteful man. Therefore, they argue, it would be wrong to presume that the 'Touting or Advertising' incidents were acts of revenge. Knowing more now about his state of mind it is quite possible that the indiscretions were prompted by his great fear of confrontation, as illustrated by his refusal to represent guilty clients in criminal cases. By taking unauthorized short cuts he thought he could achieve a quick and satisfactory result for both sides without putting clients through a protracted and expensive legal hassle. Whatever the reason it is clear that he did not consider that he had done anything seriously wrong because, less than six months after signing the undertaking, he was up to his old tricks again.

Unlike the first two occasions, no documents relating to the third incident have been found. Consequently, the following account is based solely upon the recollections of people in whom the lawyer confided shortly before his death. At that time none was aware that he had spoken to the others. So the similarities in the stories that are recounted in the following chapter would tend to confirm that the details of this case, although annoyingly sparse, are a fairly accurate record of how the lawyer landed himself in trouble yet again.

At some time during the winter of 1948-49 a local couple became involved in divorce proceedings. Hine was approached by one of the parties and agreed to take on their case. It appears that he knew the couple and became quite distressed when he learned that one was seeking a divorce. So, once again, in a sincere but unethical attempt to save a marriage, he wrote to the other party proposing a meeting between husband and wife over which he would preside and endeavour to help them resolve their differences.

When the law firm representing the other party learned that Hine had broken the undertaking, they considered they had no alternative but to file a complaint to the Law Society alleging professional malpractice. To any lawyer worth his salt the transgressions on this occasion would have been seen as two-fold. Hine's letter was a glaring example of 'Touting or Advertising' and, because a divorce action was involved, if a meeting of the kind he proposed *had* gone ahead it could have laid both parties open to charges of collusion, with possibly dire consequences for any lawyers involved. Although it has not been possible to pinpoint the precise date on which the complaint was made, there are signs that Hine's world began to fall apart during the final weeks of 1948.

In early December he was in still good spirits; penning humorous personal poems to accompany the presents he had bought for the young women who worked for him. In a letter to fellow historian James Curry he wrote cheerfully: '*Charles Lamb and His Hertfordshire* is keeping me very busy and very happy.' The two men had exchanged letters at least twice a year for more than twenty years and in due course Curry began writing a four-page reply that he had planned to send to his friend in the New Year. Then, a day or two before Christmas, he received a further communication from Hine. It was a belated Christmas greeting sent in an envelope that Curry thought might have been addressed by one of the historian's young grandsons. The writing was in large capital letters and for some reason each word had been carefully underlined in red ink. Inside was a portrait of a saintly figure sitting at a desk with a quill pen in his hand. The image was very similar to the portrait of St Vincent that Hine had chosen for his memorial tapestry, still hanging on the wall above the staircase at Willian Bury. On the back of the print was written:

'*Greetings from Hine of Hitchin.*
A rascally attorney – but your very good friend.'

Curry could not have known the significance of either the portrait or of Hine's wry description of himself. Yet he was sufficiently disturbed by the handwriting and the contents to decide not to post the reply he had written. Instead he kept it and later added a footnote: 'Somehow, I could not post this. I had a feeling Mr Hine was too ill to be tasked with his inevitable reply. He died on April 14th.'

'Do these Things go out with Life?'

WHEN *Charles Lamb and His Hertfordshire'* was published six months after Hine's death it revealed some interesting parallels in the lives of the author and his subject.

As Hine had spent twenty years ducking out of clerical duties at Hawkins & Co. to write *The History of Hitchin* so Lamb, a century earlier, had enlivened thirty tedious years in the accounts department of the East India Company by writing his sonnets and the classic *Essays of Elia*. Hine would never have claimed to match Lamb as a writer: 'No one ever wrote like him before; no one has succeeded in writing like him since,' he declares in the preface. Yet the adjectives that have frequently been applied to Lamb's essays do not look out of place when describing the historian's work: 'Whimsical, humorous and deeply human; conveying important truths about the tragicomedy of the human experience.' While Lamb's mischievous sobriquet (an anagram of 'a lie' that he pronounced 'a liar') could have slipped as easily from Hine's pen as from his own.

Then there were the shared brushes with madness. With his own fears of losing his grip on reality Hine could not have avoided being deeply affected by the disturbing problems that had blighted Lamb's life. As in 1795, when the essayist 'spent six weeks very agreeably in a mad house in Hoxton' after a Hertfordshire girl named Anna Simmons had ended their love affair. So strong were Lamb's feelings for 'the fair-haired maid' that he later dedicated his first sonnets to her. The following year, when he was twenty-one, there occurred a family tragedy that was to haunt him forever. His older sister Mary, who had nurtured his early love of literature, suffered a mental breakdown that drove her to kill their ailing mother. Worn out by working long hours as a seamstress by day and nursing a demanding invalid by night her mind eventually snapped and, on an impulse, she picked up a kitchen knife and stabbed her mother through the heart.

The matricide was declared 'an act of lunacy' and Mary was committed to an asylum, but with the help of friends Charles managed to obtain her release. He signed an undertaking to act as his sister's legal guardian and thereafter they lived together in a state of 'double singleness' for the rest of their lives. Although Mary had to return to the asylum from time to time when the mania showed signs of returning she, too, became an author in her own right. *Tales from Shakespeare*, a book for children co-written with Charles in 1807, is still being published two centuries later. Hine reminds us that whenever Mary was 'from home' it was to Hertfordshire that Lamb turned to shake off his despair:

> It was his chosen asylum of refuge in those frequent seasons when he was under 'the shadow of human imbecility,' and distracted by Mary's 'moythered brains.'

This was the county where, as a boy, Lamb had found respite from the grime of 18th century London and his strict education at Christ's Hospital charity school in Newgate. Some of *Elia's* essays contain vivid and affectionate recollections of holidays spent with his grandmother Mary Field at Widford, near Ware. Mrs Field was housekeeper and for many years sole custodian of Blakesware, a large mansion that belonged to the Plumer family and of which young Charles had the run when staying with her. There were similar enjoyable visits to a great aunt, Mrs Gladman, and her family who had a more modest farmstead across on the western side of the county at Mackery End, near Wheathampstead.

In adult life, these warm memories drew Lamb back to the county whenever he felt the need to lift his spirits. A short journey by stagecoach up the old North Road brought him to within easy reach of what he called 'my native fields.' Here he would take lodgings at an inn and spend a couple of days walking off his worries along leafy by-ways or testing his lungs on the sheep-dotted slopes of the Chiltern Hills. The very same therapy that Hine chose for himself a century later on those dark days when he felt the urge to escape the pressures of life in general and legal work in particular. Both men were known to cover as many as thirty miles a day on their therapeutic walks, a commendable enough achievement even for the long-legged historian, stepping out in his tweed suit, floppy trilby hat, leather boots and spats. Much more so, though, for the diminutive Charles Lamb, who stood well under five feet; his large head and small body perching birdlike on 'two artistically slender legs that were almost imperceptible.' A physical imbalance that caused Hine to write with admiration about his fellow 'pedestrian *in excelsis*':

> Folk smiled at the match-stick legs, the pedestrial stutter, the plantigrade motion of his puny stride; but, as a light-weight man of letters he could cover his thirty miles a day and never in Hertfordshire would he be weary . . . Charles Tween of Widford, when out walking with Lamb, would place his hands under his arms and lift him over a stile as though he were a child. According to Mrs Coe: 'Mr Lamb often had blisters but he did not seem to mind: he loved walking too much.' What an unmistakable gaiety of heart there was in this Londoner the moment he set out on those little tours into Hertfordshire which were his Grand Tours!

Although this posthumous book was received sympathetically, reviews were lukewarm. '*Hine's last book is not for everyone*,' was one headline. Fellow Elians in the Charles Lamb Society would have preferred it if the historian had stuck to his original plan to produce a slim volume that concentrated solely on Lamb's proven connections with the county. Instead, Hine took one of his leaps into the world of conjecture, hoping to create the impression that Lamb's links with the county were far stronger than they really were. Perhaps because he sensed that this would be his final book he tried to build it up to the size of his earlier five-hundred page volumes by making use of the wealth of material that had been intended for the abandoned *History of Hertfordshire*. Because most of this had little if anything to do with Lamb, he tried to justify its inclusion by decorating it with numerous quotations from the essayist and some tenuous phrases of his own:

> 'Shall we ever get to know whether Lamb really did this . . .'
> 'Had he seen it, Lamb would have found that . . .'

'Elia may have mused upon all this . . .'
Of a book: 'Had Lamb turned its pages . . .'
Of a property in Hitchin: 'This room would have won the warm approval of Lamb.'

The occasional welcome flashes of the old Hine led one reviewer to suggest that a better title for the book would have been '*Charles Lamb, Reginald Hine and Their Hertfordshire.*' Those wondering why J. M.Dent & Sons should have allowed their author to spin out of control in this way will find the reason in a letter that Hine wrote to James Curry shortly before *Confessions of an Un-Common Attorney* was published. Despite the singularly unfortunate quip contained in it, the extract suggests that, when it came to exerting editorial influence over Reginald L. Hine, his publishers had thrown in the sponge long ago:

> 26th October, 1944. Dents have been good to me. When they first of all flourished their Economy Standard Agreement in my face, and asked me to give way on this and that, I said: 'Never. Sooner than that, not only will I commit suicide, but I will write to the coroner and say why.' After that they gave me control over my own book.

* * *

Hine had just completed the Charles Lamb manuscript when he learned of the complaint against him made to the Law Society. His first reaction was to try to charm his way out of trouble, hoping that a fulsome apology to 'the other party' might persuade them to forget the matter. But, as the novelist Ursula Bloom famously wrote during *her* contretemps with Hine, 'smarming down doesn't work,' and the historian was later mortified to learn that the complaint was to go ahead. Even at this stage he felt that it was he who was the victim. A number of friends remembered him using the same hurt phrase when describing his predicament:

> 'Someone who shook me by the hand one day stabbed me in the back the next.'

Among his confidants at this time was the couple he had befriended during the war when he helped them to obtain their marriage licence. The husband, young enough to be the historian's son, found himself in the embarrassing situation of having to sit and listen while Hine, in some distress, poured out his woes:

> I don't think I was aware that he was suffering until one Saturday afternoon when my wife and I invited him round for tea. It was then that he told me he was in trouble. This came as a great shock because he was such a father figure to me. He really was a quite extraordinary man who had made a tremendous impression upon me. I don't think I can say the same thing about anyone else outside my own family circle. One has to bear in mind there was more of a generation gap in those days; I would never have called him by his Christian name and he would never have called me by mine. So when he sat himself down and said he was terribly low in spirits and there was something he really felt he had to tell me it came as a great shock. Then he told this tale of how he had been incautious enough to see both parties in a divorce suit. This was against the rules of the Law Society and somebody had reported him, so he was at risk of being struck off the roll of solicitors.

The issue rumbled on behind the scenes throughout the February and March of 1949 as the handful of lawyers involved pondered over what should be done. One Hitchin solicitor has likened the emotions generated as similar to those of a family trying to sort out the problems of a wayward son: 'I would imagine that loyalty, love, affection, frustration and sheer annoyance all played their part,' he wrote. 'Certainly at that time the idea of any external intervention in this family's affairs would have been anathema.'

Eventually, a proposal was put to Hine. If he was prepared to give up his law practice straight away there was a strong possibility that no further action would be taken. His doctor had warned him that he was on the verge of a major nervous breakdown and had been urging him to cut back on his work. As he had now reached the age of sixty-five, they suggested, the announcement of his

retirement from the Law was not likely to raise many eyebrows.
Hine took that advice and began breaking the news to friends.
'I am about to take the step pondered for the last three years
– and retire,' he wrote to Reg Cannon, editor of the *Hertfordshire
Pictorial*, 'I want to devote the rest of my days to writing.' On
March 31st his thirteen-year partnership with Reginald Hartley
came quietly to an end. However, as the young friend in whom
he had earlier confided was to discover, the episode had totally
shattered Hine's self-esteem:

> When we met later, he told me that this was such a disgrace; not
> only because of his high reputation in the legal profession, but also
> because *Confessions of an Uncommon Attorney* had become standard
> reading for budding solicitors. He felt he had let himself and his
> profession down and, altogether, his world had fallen apart. He
> said nothing about suicide but I remember he did say 'If anything
> happens to me I want you to know the facts.' At the time I didn't
> think this referred to suicide but I wondered whether he was
> heading for a nervous breakdown. That was the last time I ever saw
> him.

* * *

Suicide is discussed several times in Hine's *Confessions*. Although
over the years he lost several friends and acquaintances to the act
of self-murder, his writing contains a hint of contempt for those
who choose to escape the worries of the world in this way:

> Hardly a year, hardly a month, passes in any solicitor's office but
> some threat of suicide is made. The routine attack, by any neurotic
> woman for example, is first blandishment then, if that fails, a
> flood of tears and if the horrid lawyer still hardens his heart, she
> resolves to make an end of it all and 'you, you, you will be held
> responsible.' Self-threatened men and women are apt to live long.
> But sometimes one is mistaken and the worst befalls. Fortunate is
> that lawyer who has no such case of conscience on his mind . . . In
> the night watches I think of the doctor who took his life one hour

after receiving a private letter from me, the bitterest, most savage, that I ever penned.

Another who killed himself was Darrell Figgis, the Irish poet and novelist who had once infuriated the young Hine with his stinging comment: 'This gentleman endeavours to write in the style of Sir Thomas Browne and does not quite succeed.' Figgis later became a controversial figure in the Irish Republican movement. During the Great War he was allegedly involved in gun running and, when released from internment by the British, was elected to the first parliament of the Irish Free State. In 1924 Figgis's wife committed suicide after she discovered that he had a mistress. The following year, while staying at his London house, Figgis did the same. One senses almost a chortle of triumph in Hine's final words on this tragedy:

> The pity of it! Here was a man of heroic stature who should have died in battle. Yet he perished miserably with his head in a gas oven. My Sir Thomas Browne could have taught him to die in better style than that.

Not all the tales of suicide are treated with such flippancy. One death that had a long-lasting impact on him occurred much closer to home in 1920. Edward Smithson, a retired barrister and his wife Sarah lived at *Lewesford House*, an attractive Georgian building in Upper Tilehouse Street that once belonged to the Hitchin banker Francis Lucas. In his later years Smithson took up writing and published several books on the so-called 'Baconian theory' that some of Shakespeare's plays were really the work of Sir Francis Bacon. One afternoon he came into Hine's office is a state of great agitation. He had developed a writer's block that had left him unable to make any further progress with his work:

> As there was something that frightened me in Smithson's eyes, I walked home with him. But somehow my words returned unto me void. He would not be comforted. At the door of his lovely house I said: 'Take my advice. Forget all about Francis Bacon for a time.

Get some fun out of the plays. Does it really matter who wrote them? Promise me to laugh your way through *Henry IV, Part I*, this very night.' That was the last I saw of Edward Smithson. He shot himself a few hours later. The saddest thing about this tragedy was that he left no letter of explanation or farewell.

To cope with her grief Edward's widow turned to some of the country's most respected psychics for help and (according to Hine, at least) achieved impressive results. In his short profile *Sarah Smithson (1844-1928)* in *Hitchin Worthies*, and also in his *Confessions*, he expresses a firm belief that Sarah not only made regular contact with her dead husband at these seances, she was also able to plan the remaining years of her life guided by his advice:

> It is a pity that she required me to destroy the records of his communications. Some were of an impersonal character and might with advantage have been filed in the archives of the Society for Psychical Research of which she was a member. Particularly Edward's description (she showed me thirty pages of it one day) of the natural history of the other world, and his amazement and joy at finding the daylight split up into its prismatic colours. The particular problem with which he was devoting his time, or rather his eternity, concerned the behaviour of ants in the spiritual world and unfortunately it was divulged that he was being assisted in his studies by a woman of whom Mrs Smithson strongly disapproved. I well remember her consulting me as if I ought to be able to do something practical in the matter. It was a curious predicament, and one for which, as a lawyer, I could find no precedent in the books.

These experiences all helped to strengthen Hine's belief in an after-life and that it is possible to communicate with those who have 'gone before.' In the final months, as he wrestled with the prospect of his own mortality, he became more desperate than ever for assurance that something, someone, was waiting for him beyond the veil. As the real-life nightmares began to close in around him like the demons in his dreams, his candle-lit study at Willian Bury became a final place of refuge to share with Charles Lamb, the kindred spirit with whom he had formed such a close affinity.

His book recalls how, on the evening of 27th December 1948 Hine climbed into his world-weary banger *Sir Henry* and set off across the county to Widford village, where the essayist had spent his boyhood holidays. With *Elia's* romantic descriptions of Blakesware ringing in his ears he parked and set off in the wintry moonlight to find Lamb's old haunts. After struggling through a wilderness of briars that covered the site where the mansion had stood he reached a little bridge over the River Ash where Charles and Mary Lamb had once sailed their model boats:

> 'Where is Elia?' My cry, added to that of poet Clare, went wailing down the night . . . There was not the ghost of a ghost to be seen. It was here in twilight I had come a twelvemonth before and had afterwards been driven to admit: 'We do not catch sight of him because we are so slow. With a kingfisher flash he skims the surface of the stream and is away.' . . . . He never cared greatly for the society of what he called good people. Perhaps it is only the good people who are privileged to show themselves, to 'appear' to the living after death? Though I could not behold him, I could hear him and it seemed as though he walked beside me in those shades.

These were not the last words that Hine wrote about Charles Lamb. Shortly after the manuscript had been delivered to the publishers the historian posted them one of his notoriously late additions. It was a short poem intended for the final page of the book. This time, Martin Dent put his foot down and returned the poem with a letter of regret. A few days later, as the historian began to tidy up his affairs, he sent the poem to one of his literary friends in the hope that one day it would be published. The note that he wrote to accompany the poem says a great deal:

> My dear friend,
> 1. Keep this for me too. Dents think it will not do for my new book.

2. But I like it. It ought to see the light of day sometime.

3. I am very low spirited and riddled with nerves, but look to see you at 3.45 tomorrow Saturday.

Yours, R.L.H.

Martin Dent had, in fact, rejected Hine's last piece of creative writing; writing that reflected his eagerness to know what lay in wait for him on 'the other side.' He had first called the poem *'L'Envoi,'* a title frequently given to verses at the end of a literary composition to convey a moral; but before posting it to his friend he had made a hand-written change that altered the whole meaning. *'L'Envoi'* had been replaced by *'Valediction'* thus making his poem 'a farewell speech.' Beneath the title Hine had also written a telling line from one of Lamb's own poems: *'And do these things go out with life?'*

i.

Say, once-blithe spirit, is it well with thee?
How farest thou, Elia, in Eternity?
Say does thy ghost-ship walk and laugh and jest,
Or, stretched on asphodel, art thou at rest?
Sweet sun and sky, footpath and hillside walks,
Flickering fancies, frolic of fireside talks,
Ingle-nook whimsies, genial-hearted rhymes,
Thy 'bosom-cronie' books of elder times,
The gay remembrance of a stolen kiss -
Are these denied thee in the realm of bliss?
Do these go out with life?

ii.

Say, is it true what thou wast wont to dread?
No bookstalls and no inns! No tables spread
With bubble and squeak, dumplings and sucking-pig,
Tankards of porter, muscadine and fig?
What cheer, departed Charles? Can the dead play
Cribbage and whist? And what are trumps today?
Is Manning with thee? Martin, Leigh Hunt and 'Col'?

Where is that 'jovial crew' thy works extol?
Speak you with Hester now, thy dark-haired girl?
With fair-haired Anna is thy heart a-whirl?
      Or Love itself, does that go out with life?

iii.

Not yet to thine unknown and silent shore
May we embark. Heartsick we must explore
Our dregs of fate: 'the dark condition
Of blind humanity': that low perdition
That men endure bereft of peace and joy.
We miss thee, Elia. In earth's alloy
There was no man more brave, more true. You spoke
And wisdom smiled. A stuttered joke
Might 'scald like tears', or set the mad heart free.
We laugh no more, we breed of lesser folk
      The world of wit went out with thee.

CHARLES LAMB

A version of the etching from Daniel Maclise's
Portrait Gallery of Illustrious Literary Characters, 1830-38
used by Hine in his *Charles Lamb & His Hertfordshire.*

[13]
Crossing the Owl's Bridge

ONLY DURING the last fortnight of historian's life did StellaWhite, the young nanny at Willian Bury, become aware that something was wrong. By the April of 1949 she had been there a year, staying on as Florence's companion whenever the grandchildren were abroad. Now, the whole family was together again. Bill McEwen had taken some Easter leave and returned from Sudan to join Felicity and the boys at their grandmother's house. Having been built for wealthy clergymen with large families the old Georgian rectory could easily accommodate the sudden influx of visitors. Stella had her own room adjacent to the nursery where she ate with the children during the day, joining the adults for dinner each evening in the main dining room. Her time there had been very happy:

> I got on very well with Mrs Hine and have memories of warm
> summer days and the most wonderful picnics that sometimes
> included ice-cooled flasks of 'Gin and It' (gin and vermouth) in
> the hamper. She was extremely kind to me. When the children
> were not there we often went out to dinner at Letchworth Hall, an
> exciting experience for a young person in those rather austere days.
> As a couple, she and Reggie were totally different. While she was
> very upright he was far more outgoing and jolly; always making
> jokes. He enjoyed showing people his books and antiques and
> one day took me into his office to see a marvellous collection of
> Victorian Valentine cards.
> He loved his grandsons dearly but I wouldn't say he was very
> close to them. He didn't play cricket in the garden with them or
> anything like that. One has to remember that he was well into
> his sixties by then and I think he found them too boisterous. For
> this reason the small enclosed garden outside the kitchen window
> became known as 'Grandpa's Garden' where the children were
> not allowed and where he would sometimes sit and read. Most

evenings he would have dinner with us and then disappear to his study immediately afterwards to resume work on his manuscripts.

Stella had no recollections of tension or arguments during the days leading up to Hine's death, suggesting that no one was yet aware of the crisis he was facing. The first she heard of it was from Hine himself:

One day shortly before his death he took me into the dining room and told me that he had had to resign from the partnership because a complaint alleging malpractice had been made against him to the Law Society. Divorce was very rare in those days and I think he was trying to patch up a marriage and had approached the other partner when he should not have done. He was particularly upset because someone had, as he put it, shaken him by the hand one day and stabbed him in the back the next. He just couldn't bear it and resigned straight away. He was so miserable. Then, one day when Mrs Hine was away, I found him busy clearing out his bedroom and he said something that seemed very strange at the time. He said: 'Stella, if anything should ever happen to me, would you tell Mrs Hine that there are some Lucas water colours on the top of my wardrobe.' I said: 'Oh my goodness ! I'm sure I won't be here when that happens.' Sadly, the day was not far off when I *did* have to tell her.

The recollections of Stella and of the Hitchin couple in the previous chapter suggest that, having decided to end his life, Hine guessed there would be an attempt to conceal the real reasons why he had been driven to take this fatal step. So he made a point of giving his version of events to a number of younger people whom he knew he could trust. He also confided in one of the Pyman family. Joannie, the daughter of Florence's elder brother Frank, lived in a stone cottage overlooking the sea at Swanage in Dorset. One weekend she was surprised when 'Uncle Reg' arrived unexpectedly and proceeded to unburden his problems to her. Like Stella, Joannie listened sympathetically but there was little she or anyone else could do to relieve the historian's anguish.

'Self-threatened men and women are apt to live long' Hine wrote in his *Confessions*, implying that people who go round advertising their suicide rarely do it. With those seriously intent on self-harm it is the reverse. Countless families who have experienced such a tragedy remember loved ones behaving apparently quite normally sometimes only minutes before committing the act. It was to be the same with Hine. As he set about clearing his office at Hartley & Hine, none of the secretaries detected anything out of the ordinary. There is a studied nonchalance (and a small white lie) in this note that accompanied some papers that Hine passed on to a fellow antiquarian on March 26th:

> In my office today (spring cleaning) I found the enclosed which were (if I remember) given to me by Miss Wilshere. They should, undoubtedly, join your other county treasures. Let me know they have safely arrived.

The publisher Martin Dent found Hine as jovial and enthusiastic as ever when he called at the Bury to discuss some late amendments to the Charles Lamb book less than twenty-four hours before its author killed himself. Neither did Stella White notice anything unusual when the historian appeared for the last time at breakfast.

Maundy Thursday, April 14th, was dry and sunny, prompting a discussion among the adults about whether it was warm enough to take the children on a picnic. As their grandfather returned to his study to work Stella remembered him saying he would be unable to come because he had 'arranged to see some ladies.' Shortly after that Florence, Felicity and Bill McEwen left the house to drive into Hitchin to do some shopping. About noon, Stella was in the nursery with the children when a car suddenly swung into the driveway being driven at speed. A woman jumped out, ran up to the house and rang the bell. Stella opened the front door to find the distraught figure of Margaret Gavin-Jones, a prominent member of the Letchworth community and one of Florence's closest friends:

She was in a terrible state. I asked what was the matter but all she would say was 'Oh my dear! Something terrible has happened. Something terrible.' She kept repeating this but would not say what it was. I told her that Mrs Hine would be home shortly and invited her in to wait. A few moments later I heard the family car on the drive and went out quickly to try to tell them that all was not well but as soon as I mentioned Mrs Gavin-Jones' name Mrs Hine exclaimed 'Oh how lovely! I haven't seen her for ages!' As she hurried ahead into the house I was just able to warn Bill and Felicity that something dreadful had happened and they went quickly indoors.

I did not hear Mrs Gavin-Jones break the news because I had to return to the children to make sure that they remained in the nursery until their parents were ready to see them. Some time later Mr Hine's partner Mr Hartley called to confirm that he had indeed died after falling in front of a train. The awful thing was that, as they were driving home from shopping, Mrs Hine had had to slow down at the station to allow an ambulance to come out of the approach road. Only later did she realise that it must have contained her husband's body.

The condition of Hine's remains dictated that an early funeral was essential. Usually, to enable burial to take place, an inquest is opened briefly for the coroner to hear evidence of identification and cause of death. It is then adjourned for the full hearing to take place at a later date. For reasons known only to them, those arranging Hine's inquest decided instead to get the whole thing over as quickly as possible.

Information gathered over the next two days revealed that the historian had left the Bury at about 10.30 a.m. and driven down the hill to Hitchin Station, parking his car in its usual spot on the forecourt. At the booking office he bought a return ticket for the 11.12 fast train to King's Cross, the train he usually took whenever he went to London. In the booking hall he had bumped into a friend, Matthew Bevan of Stotfold, who was there to meet relatives arriving on a slow train from Cambridge that was due to arrive before the London train, at 10.48. With time to spare, the two men walked through the subway to Platform Two, where southbound trains stop, and continued their conversation sitting on a bench near the entrance to the station buffet. 'It was a perfectly normal conversation,' Mr Bevan said later. As they chatted the platform gradually filled with passengers; families going away for Easter, others on a day trip to the capital. So the area was fairly crowded when the 10.48 slow train trundled into the station, travelling at about fifteen-miles-an hour.

At that moment, and without a word of explanation, Hine suddenly stood up, hurried to the platform's edge and flung himself onto the track in front of the train. The fireman on the engine saw it happen and so did a porter but Hine moved so quickly that neither man could have stopped him or the train in time. 'Perhaps it was the hideous whine of its brakes as it began to grind to a halt that made him rise to the final challenge,' Basil Donne-Smith wrote many years later. 'For with a tremendous gesture, throwing life itself to the winds, he rushed (in a strange way almost gloriously) to his quietus. Men die, just as they live, in many and various ways. Some are loath to go; others are eager to depart. Yet all are brought at the end to a common and most merciful salvation from all pain. For so he giveth his beloved, sleep.'

* * *

When the inquest was held at Hitchin hospital on Easter Saturday morning Matthew Bevan, the train crew and the porter all described what they had witnessed of the historian's last moments. Dr Marshall Gilbertson, who had been called to the scene by the police, said the historian would have died instantly from multiple injuries to the brain. His partner, Dr Howard Dumere, after revealing that he had been treating Hine for threatened nervous breakdowns on and off for thirteen years, added: 'He had been depressed for some weeks and at the time of his death was under treatment for recent depression. I had advised him to give up either his professional work or his writing and on March 31st he actually retired from his profession.'

The evidence was sufficient for the deputy coroner George Shillitoe to record a verdict that the historian had deliberately killed himself while the balance of his mind was disturbed. Not a word was mentioned about the complaint to the Law Society. Perhaps it was to avoid this subject that Mr Shillitoe decided not to reveal the details of a note that Hine had left for him. He said only that the contents left him in no doubt as to 'the situation' and he did not see how any useful purpose could be served by making the note public. Thus, at his own inquest, Hine was denied a final opportunity to put his side of the story. In fact, this was not unusual. Even today, to avoid causing unnecessary distress to families, most coroners tend to refer to the details of a suicide note only in general terms. However, there were some aspects of the Hine inquest that a present-day coroner found quite extraordinary.

The Hitchin-born solicitor Andrew Haigh was a Deputy Coroner in Hertfordshire for many years before being appointed Coroner for Staffordshire South. He explained that, despite various proposals for major reforms over the years, the law relating to inquests is in essence very similar to what it was in 1949. But because coroners are *independent* judicial officers there is (and probably always has been) considerable variation in the way each individual would deal with the deaths reported to them:

What I find most remarkable is the time-scale. For the death to have occurred on Maundy Thursday and the full inquest with several professional witnesses to take place on the morning of Easter Saturday is absolutely incredible. Whilst inquests in the 1940s may have been a lot quicker in all respects, it does look to me as though people would have had to put themselves out considerably for it to take place when it did. Nowadays it is more likely that the inquest would have been opened on the Tuesday or Wednesday after Easter with the full hearing being held several weeks or even a few months later.

Another interesting point is that the inquest appears to have been held without a jury. Even today coroners vary in their approach on this subject; some railway deaths may have juries others may not. As I understand the situation, the basic provision is that a jury is necessary if death results from an accident where notice needs to be given to a Government department. Recent guidelines have suggested that railway suicides should have juries but there is no clear authority for this. If anything juries were more common in 1949 than they are now. While the law at the time may not have bound Mr Shillitoe to have a jury I am a little surprised that he did not.

Yet, imagining himself in a situation similar to that of George Shillitoe, Andrew Haigh said he was not sure that he would have read out the full contents of the note either; particularly if it had included a list of reasons why the dead man had decided to take his own life. (One might also speculate that if Hine's note had repeated his recent allegation that he had been 'stabbed in the back', reading that out in court could have opened a very large can of worms!) Although Mr Shillitoe undoubtedly steered an impartial judicial course that day, it was for him a difficult situation. As a lawyer, he would have known of the trouble Hine was in; as a descendant of the famous Quaker Shillitoes, about whom the historian had written so much so well, he must also have held Hine in high regard and would not have wanted to exacerbate a tragedy that had already shaken the community to its very roots.

The one problem caused by not reading out the note was that it led to half a century of speculation and rumours about the 'real' reason that Hine killed himself. These have suggested that he had been diagnosed with incurable cancer, that he had been caught 'fiddling the books' at Hartley & Hine and that his wife was planning to leave him. None was true. The one credible theory suggests he had been on his way to be interviewed by the Law Society's Disciplinary Panel that Thursday morning. The fact that he had purchased a return ticket to King's Cross suggests that he set out fully intending to go to London but suddenly decided that the prospect of facing an humiliating interview by his peers was an ordeal he was not prepared to face at any price.

Unfortunately it has not been possible to verify this theory.

The Law Society's archives hold no records of complaints and disciplinary proceedings dealt with during the immediate post-war period. Neither, at that time, was there a central storage system for inquest papers. So, after nearly sixty years, it seems highly unlikely that Hine's note to George Shillitoe will have survived. Evidence given at later Hertfordshire inquests is now more accessible; since 1960 their papers have been stored in the county archive at Hertford.

There is a cruelly ironic postscript to this tragedy. If Hine *was* on his way to the Law Society that day he would have learned that, as he had since given up practising law, they would not be taking the complaint any further. This fact was confirmed in a letter that arrived at his home a few days after his death – a death that certainly flew in the face of the romantic demise that he had imagined for himself. In the final paragraph of *Confessions* he relished the bliss of ending his life amid the peaceful ruins of Minsden Chapel:

> To sink down into this cool quietness of trees, to be softly surrounded with gleaming fantasies of foliage, to dream the last dreams in this haunt of wild flowers, bright-hearted birds and those sweet-minded things which live where silence is. This would be not to die but to pass deliciously from peace to peace.

If only that had happened. If he had been found at Minsden having succumbed to an overdose of barbiturate then in all probability his suicide would have seemed somehow more acceptable to the community. What people found so hard to forgive was the hideous and selfish exit that he chose; selfish, because it traumatised not only his family and friends but numerous others – in particular the train crew and those who had to recover the body. If he did plan his death as a public act of revenge to shock his accusers then 'unforgivable' might be considered a suitable adjective. However, the genuine remorse that Hine had shown when telling various friends of the trouble he was in suggests the opposite; that neither the method nor the moment was premeditated.

Bipolar disorder causes more suicides than any other mental illness. Of those who have it but are not receiving treatment, half are reckoned to attempt suicide and a fifth of those who try it succeed. Hine's death also shares certain similarities with that of a civil servant who ended his life in 1996 after being hounded mercilessly by the news media. The man's widow wrote later: 'He had suffered from depression, but it was the publicity, the loss of honour and his good name that drove him to suicide. The black hole of despair and tunnel vision that says: "Everyone would be better off without me" blots out compassion for loved ones and causes temporary insanity.' If Hine *was* on his way to the Law Society's offices that day, his mind would have been in turmoil as he sat on the station bench and struggled to conduct a conversation with Matthew Bevan. As pleasantries were exchanged he would have been thinking only of the interview that lay ahead and the possibility that, despite his recent resignation from Hartley & Hine, his name could still be removed from the solicitors' roll; that he, too, could be about to suffer 'the publicity, the loss of honour and his good name'.

Having made up his mind earlier to end his life, he had already written a note for the coroner explaining his action but had still not decided precisely where or when to do it. Basil Donne-Smith suggested that the screeching brakes of the arriving train were the catalyst that caused his mind to snap. This theory is now strengthened by an unusual and intriguing story that has come to light. As with certain passages in Hine's own books the following scenario of his death is based upon 'informed speculation.' Had he been writing this book he would undoubtedly have encouraged his readers to look further to find more mystical reasons for his suicide. One that deserves consideration is the credible story of a ghost that had haunted him on and off since the days of his youth and which, according to friends, reappeared shortly before his death.

* * *

Of all the living creatures associated with mythology and folklore few are more mystical than the owl. One of the world's oldest surviving vertebrate animals, its remains have been found in fossils that go back sixty million years and it is one of the few birds to appear in prehistoric cave paintings. Throughout the world different civilisations have looked upon it variously in admiration, fear and wonder. The ancient Greeks saw it as a symbol of good fortune, the Romans as an omen of impending disaster. In Shakespeare's *Julius Caesar*, it is an owl that presages the ruler's death:

> *And yesterday the bird of night did sit, even at noonday,*
> *Upon the market place, hooting and shrieking.*

Similarly, among the North American Indian tribes owls are either revered for harbouring the souls of the recently departed or cursed as harbingers of sickness and death. Some tribes actually refer to death as 'crossing the owl's bridge.'

In England it is the Barn Owl that has been held in awe down the centuries. This majestic creature is known also as the White Owl, because of its ghostly face and white under plumage and the Screech Owl, because of its eerie night call. 'White Owls screech horribly as they fly along,' wrote the 18th-century naturalist Gilbert White. 'The bird also snores and hisses in a tremendous manner and these menaces well answer the intention of intimidating, for I have known a whole village up in arms on such an occasion, imagining the churchyard to be full of goblins and spectres.' The bird has another trick that it employs when threatened or alarmed. It lowers its head and moves it from side to side making loud snapping noises with its mandibles. Reginald Hine experienced this close at hand when, in his youth, he shot and maimed a barn owl on his father's farm at Newnham. It was this incident that he later blamed for a recurring nightmare in which he tried to fend off hordes of demons with a shotgun that would not fire:

> It is significant that that impotence came upon me after I shot
> a gigantic barn owl in the back meadow of my old home at

Newnham Hall. The bird (but owls are something more than birds) was a long time dying, and it glared at me with such ferocity of expression that its eyes will haunt me for the remainder of my days.

The fact that the bird 'was a long time dying' can mean only one thing. Having failed to make a clean kill Hine left the owl to die in agony. He was probably appalled by what he had done, yet lacked the stomach to end the bird's suffering with a *coup de grâce*. It is not hard to visualise the guilty lad creeping back into the meadow to see if the creature's suffering had ended, only to find it lying there, still alive and panting noisily with the pain. Its magnificent wings, spanning nearly three feet, beating helplessly on the grass with each futile attempt at escape; the beautiful plumage just beginning to show signs of the blood that oozed steadily from the shattered body beneath. And all the time the creature's head dipped instinctively from side to side in its defensive mode. Worst of all were the deep, dark eyes that focussed accusingly on their killer accompanied by the rasping *'snap snap ... snap snap'* from its throat, a sound that bore an uncanny resemblance to a human voice.

As our respect for Life increases with age, what man does not experience pangs of remorse over the beautiful things destroyed in his youth through cruel and pointless acts of violence? The more so for Hine, whose acute depression was by this time causing symptoms of psychosis. Symptoms that took the feelings of guilt over his legal transgressions to such profound depths that they revived the creature whose cruel death had first pricked his conscience half a century earlier. As he had admitted, owls are something more than birds. Indeed, such is their reputation for sagacity that when a group are gathered together they are known as 'a wisdom' or 'a Parliament.'

Hine did not deliberately seek out the barn owl that came to him during his last days. In the midst of all his troubles, it had suddenly turned up and he was quite perplexed by its presence. Two independent sources recalled how, in the last week of his life, the historian had puzzled friends by asking if they thought that owls could communicate with human beings. When they asked cautiously why he wanted to know, he said simply: 'Because I have an owl that speaks to me now, quite frequently.' From this sad revelation it is not unreasonable to assume that when the 10.48 slow train from Cambridge was grinding noisily to a halt at Hitchin Station on April 14th 1949, it was not the screech of its brakes that Reginald Hine heard. It was the screech of the barn owl. And when he heard it he knew what he had to do. The time to cross the owl's bridge had come.

Thomas Bewick's wood-engraving of the Barn Owl
for his *History of British Birds*, 1797.

[14]
Living On

HAPPENING AS IT DID over Easter, Hine's suicide caused a number of problems for the Vicar of Hitchin, Canon Edward Kempe. During this busy and most solemn period of the Church calendar he was asked to prepare a fitting Christian farewell for a man who some parishioners now regarded as a transgressor. He had to devise a funeral for a much-loved citizen who had championed his town and parish church for half a century and yet had chosen to die by 'laying violent hands upon himself.' In 1949 not only was self-murder a sin in the eyes of the Church, it was still classified as a crime under English law. Twelve years were to pass before it was finally decriminalised by the Suicide Act of 1961.

Before the 19th century both Church and State had abhorred suicides with equal fervour. Draconian penalties included confiscation of their property and denial of a Christian burial. Often, self-murderers were buried at a crossroads with a stake driven through the body. Eventually, to allow bereaved families to claim a Christian burial for their loved ones, coroners and inquest juries began to add saving riders to their verdicts to indicate that the suicides had killed themselves 'while of unsound mind.' Even so, this more compassionate approach did not arrive overnight; a good illustration of the Church of England's slow acceptance of change can be found in the 1925 edition of their *Prayer Book Dictionary*:

> SUICIDE: The first rubric at the head of the Burial Service runs as follows: 'Here is to be noted that the Office ensuing is not to be used for any that die unbaptised, or excommunicate, or have laid violent hands upon themselves.' Christianity has always regarded a suicide as excommunicate in that he deliberately destroys that life which God has given him to cherish, and which Christ came to redeem. The alarming increase in suicides in recent years is

49. The tall figure of Hine (*right*) at the ceremony when Ralph Sanders relinquished his ownership of Cottered village green to the Parish Council.

50. A group of cycling enthusiasts photographed by T.B. Latchmore outside his studios in Brand Street, Hitchin *c.*1890. The glass roof of the studio is just visible.

51 - 52. Hitchin from the top of Windmill Hill. A drawing by the etcher, illustrator and architect, F.L. Griggs RA, son of a Hitchin baker. Possibly an unused study for Herbert Tompkins' *Highways & Byways in Hertfordshire*, 1902. Twelve volumes of this extensive county series were illustrated by Griggs.

53. An early view of Leys Avenue, Letchworth Garden City.

54. Hine (*foreground*) listening as Viscount Lytton of Knebworth performs the opening ceremony at a garden party in Broadway, Letchworth. Behind Lord Lytton is Arthur Brunt, author of *Pageant of Letchworth*.

55. Bernard Shaw, booked by Hine to speak at a librarians' convention at Letchworth, annoyed the forty delegates by abandoning his advertised lecture on 'Libraries and the English Language' to speak on a totally different subject. 'Sometimes the lot of a chairman can be hard,' Hine wrote later. 'Some of the abuse was directed at me for not calling Shaw to order.'

56. Mrs Margaret Harvey. Councillor, magistrate and close friend of Hine.

57. Hine's last studio portrait taken a few months before his death

58. Fifty years on. The Hine family's nanny, Mrs Stella Edwards, photographed during a return visit to Willian Bury in 2005.

59. Stella's three young charges – (L to R) Michael, Andrew and William McEwen – in 1949.

60. April 1949. A small cairn of flints marks the spot at Minsden Chapel where the historian's ashes were scattered.

61. Hine's gravestone is still where his grandsons (*below*) re-set it in 1983.

62. The McEwen brothers and their families pictured during their weekend at Minsden when they reclaimed the site of their grandfather's grave.

63. The old Free School that was demolished to make way for road improvements at the top of Tilehouse Street, Hitchin. A drawing by J.C. Buckler, 1832.

64. The site in September 1952 when townspeople gathered for the official opening of the Hine Memorial Garden

65. Before the ceremony Florence Hine (*left*) speaks with the Vicar of Hitchin the Revd G.N.O. Walsh. The Lord Lieutenant of Hertfordshire, David Bowes Lyon, is with the historian's daughter Felicity and brother Eric Hine.

66. The Chairman of Hitchin U.D.C., Councillor F.O. Foster (*left*) and the Lord Lieutenant listen as the Vicar leads the short service of dedication.

due to a diminishing religious sensitiveness - also largely to the
jury's frequent verdict of 'while of unsound mind' which entitles
the relatives of the suicide to claim Christian burial for him. The
rubric in the Prayer Book obviously did not contemplate that
large numbers of those who 'lay violent hands upon themselves'
would be classed as insane, or the wording would in all probability
have been different... The refusal of Christian burial must have
had a deterrent effect where Christianity was a vital force. It is
found that, where religious belief is definite and its hold upon the
people is strong, there is less incentive to self-destruction. The clear
teaching given in the prayer book, if carefully imparted, would do
much to reduce the number of suicides.

In Hine's case, there was an added complication in that he had
asked for his body to be cremated, and crematoria were still few
and far between; the two nearest to Hitchin were at Cambridge
and Golders Green in north London, both about thirty miles
away. Even though most places had closed for the Bank Holiday,
Canon Kempe and the family managed to draw up a plan that
would enable the funeral to go ahead on Easter Tuesday. That
morning Chenery's the Hitchin undertakers would take the coffin
containing Hine's remains to Golders Green for cremation. They
would wait there until the ashes had cooled and then bring them
back to Hertfordshire to be scattered that afternoon at the ruins
of Minsden Chapel, in accordance with the historian's wishes.
While the cremation was taking place a service would be held
at St Mary's Church but because Hine's remains were not in
the church the event would have to be classified as a Memorial
Service.

When Florence, Felicity and the rest of the family arrived,
the great nave of the church was already packed. In the pews
behind them sat row upon row of the friends and professional
acquaintances that had been a part of Hine's two lives; lawyers,
historians and academics from all over Hertfordshire, from
London and further afield. Town and county councillors shared
pews with parish clerks from the remote villages and hamlets of
the county. Any spare seat was quickly taken by one of the scores

of individuals who had turned up to pay their respects simply
because they were ardent admirers of the man and his work. It
was from these ranks that voices were later heard complaining
that the service had not done Hine justice. They pointed out that,
although it was described as a memorial service, neither the clergy
nor anyone else had come forward to pay tribute to Hine's life and
work. The sad fact was that, although the historian was entitled
to a Christian burial, there was still a strict ruling within the
Church that those who died by their own hand should not have
a eulogy spoken at their funeral. So the only intimate concession
that Canon Kempe felt able to make was a reading of the well-
meant but rather rambling prayer that Hine had composed for the
concluding paragraph of his *History of Hitchin*:

> Listen! There is St. Mary's bell; and it ringeth to evensong. Let us
> make haste, for there is a prayer to be said in the Trinity chapel;
> and not only by myself, but by all good citizens of this town, and
> by all those who are piously disposed amongst the readers of this
> book: 'Eternal and ever-blessed God, who hast made us the heirs
> of many ages, and set us in the midst of many brethren, deepen
> our gratitude for Thy blessings as we have received them from our
> fathers, our benefactors and our friends. May we never forget the
> kindness which surrounds us in the present, nor be unmindful of
> the treasures we inherit from the past; but, having a lively sense of
> our debt to the brethren and a loving remembrance of departed
> generations, may we reverently carry forward the work of the ages
> and daily endeavour, as faithful stewards, to enrich the same by a
> good conversation and a godly life.'

The omission of a proper eulogy prompted a number of the
congregation to write to the local newspapers expressing their
dismay. This letter appeared in the *Hertfordshire Express*:

> The memorial service to Mr Hine, held in the old church with a
> softened sun shining through the windows and the Easter flowers,
> had a quiet setting of rest and triumph. But there should have
> been a reference to the life of so great an historian, a mastermind
> and a great friend with a splendid character, probably the greatest

benefactor Hitchin has even known. Thousands of people in
Hitchin and beyond knew him as the friend with a cheerful smile,
a pat on the back and untold deeds of kindness. We are happy to
acknowledge our gratitude and appreciation.'

A friend who was at the service recalled: 'I seem to remember
that Hine's name was mentioned only once, just at the very
beginning. Although the service was quite long the whole thing
seemed terribly low key. It was cold and impersonal, as though
they wanted to suppress all thought of the man – almost as if they
wanted to get shot of him'.

Afterwards the Hine and Pyman families drove out to Minsden
Chapel for a final private ceremony at which Florence scattered her
husband's ashes on the chancel floor of the hilltop ruin. Clearing
a space among the weeds and wild flowers the family marked
the site with a roughly built 'cairn,' using flints that had once
formed part of the chapel wall and planting a few polyanthuses
within it. In due course Florence was given permission to lay a
proper memorial stone at the site. However, when the family
attempted to hang the much-vaunted Hine Memorial Tapestry
in St Vincent's Church, Newnham, (the historian's birthplace)
they ran into opposition from an unexpected quarter.

Before the tapestry could be hung in the church Florence
had first to obtain permission from the Bishop of St Albans.
A 'notice of intent' was pinned on the church door to give
parishioners the opportunity to object to the proposal and, as
none was forthcoming, diocesan approval was granted. In due
course Florence made arrangements for the tapestry and its hefty
frame to be taken down from the wall over the staircase at Willian
Bury and delivered to the church. Only then did it transpire that
there had been an objector all along, in the person of the Vicar of
Newnham, the Reverend Victor Roos. Although he appears not
to have made his views known to the Bishop, Mr Roos shocked
his parishioners by suddenly declaring that, because of the manner
in which Hine had ended his life, he did not think it would be
appropriate to have a memorial to him in the church. He would
therefore not allow the tapestry to be displayed.

Newnham's life-long resident Mrs Sheila Rosendale recalled the sense of outrage felt by parishioners over their vicar's peremptory action: 'After making his pronouncement the silly man deliberately left the tapestry standing on the floor in a dark corner, hidden from sight behind a door. It remained there for several years, collecting dust and cobwebs. Everyone in the village was very unhappy about it, not least the vicar's wife Winnie; so we decided to keep working on him and eventually he relented and allowed it to be hung in the church on a nice sunlit wall, where it has stayed ever since.'

Although the Church's hidebound rules relating to suicide robbed Hine of the send-off he would have been given had he died in any other way, his numerous friends and admirers were quick to record their tributes. Florence and her family were inundated with letters of condolence, and others filled many columns of the county newspapers and magazines. The strength of feeling and the affection shown suggested that, even if the touting and advertising affair *had* become public knowledge, the public's reaction would have been more of amusement and forgiveness rather than outrage. It was not Hine the imperfect lawyer whose loss they mourned but Hine the charismatic historian; the man who had brought a thousand years of local history back to life and, in so doing, had given them renewed pride in their town. Dr Richenda Scott, his former research assistant who went on to become an historian in her own right, wrote later: 'I was in Hitchin during the week following his death and never have I experienced such a sense of a whole community mourning.' Basil Donne-Smith summed up the sense of loss in verse:

IN MEMORIAM R.L.H.
Obit Maundy Thursday 1949

We came together when we heard,
We sought each other out and said:
'There is a trouble on the town,
The day is darkened … he is dead.'

So oft he schooled us, we forgot
At times, the love his ardour hid.
'He thinks he owns the place,' we said.
And, in the truest sense, he did.

The gold and scarlet of the past
He brought to shame our pallid age.
And who of us, today, is not
The richer for this heritage?

Rest now, Great Heart, those mourn for you
Whom our dull vision cannot see.
A Baliol shall watch your bier,
A Chapman sing your threnody.

The haven of a Quaker calm
Harbours at last your questing soul.
For you, across the Langley fields,
The legend bells of Minsden toll.

For us the Spring on Windmill Hill
Will be the less, till we recall
That in the little town below
We gaze on his memorial.

*   *   *

Despite the fact that they had led virtually separate lives for thirty years, Florence's respect for her husband's achievements as an historian never once diminished. Partly to cope with her grief she busied herself with the preparation of a final literary tribute. Helped by her friends Richenda Scott and Mildred Bozman she began selecting material for a book modelled on Hine's earlier volumes and containing a miscellany of his unpublished work. From the chaos of his study she salvaged a selection of material ranging from a pithy essay on the law and swearing to a study of the life and art of his old friend F.L. Griggs. She also found a little-known tale of his discovery of an iron fiddle that had been made and played by the tinker John Bunyan before his evangelistic days. Neatly titled *Relics of An Un-Common Attorney* the book was published by Dent in 1951, and sold well.

Particularly revealing is a fulsome introductory memoir written by Richenda Scott, his one-time *protégée*. It encapsulates all the feelings of those who believed that, as an historian, he could do no wrong: 'Reginald Hine always seemed to me like some Renaissance scholar reincarnate. Full of the zest of life, eagerly questing after the beautiful and the rare – in furnishings, or pictures, or books, or in people; walking with a gallant swagger through the difficult and often perilous ways of this world, until that last dark moment when the shadows overcame him.' Dr. Scott had no doubt that Hine's human approach to his work, coupled with his ability to 'think himself' into the minds of his subjects, placed him among the leading historian-philosophers of his day. 'I remember many years ago someone saying to me what a pity it was that he should be confining his energies to the study of parochial records when he had the gifts and the vision to write a stirring book on some great theme of national or world significance; as Gibbon chose the decline of the Roman Empire for *his* field. . .'

In that same year of 1951 the historian's writing was brought vividly to life for the Festival of Britain. As North Hertfordshire's contribution to the national celebrations Hitchin Civic and Arts Association commissioned one of England's best-known pageant masters, Cyril Swinson of St Albans, to write and produce a pageant charting nine hundred years of the town's history. Performed against the backdrop of Hitchin Priory, the event featured 1,300 performers with many more townsfolk working in support groups behind the scenes. Following a gala opening night attended by The Queen, the pageant was seen by more than 16,000 people; the largest theatrical spectacle ever staged in the area. In the programme Swinson wrote: 'Most of the episodes are based upon incidents recorded in Reginald Hine's excellent and exhaustive books . . . In acknowledging my gratitude to him for making my task so easy, my only regret is that he did not live to write the pageant himself.'

As the trauma of Hine's death began to recede, thoughts turned to providing a suitable memorial. Almost by providence an opportunity occurred during a council re-development scheme that, ironically, would have appalled the man whose life they were seeking to commemorate. A road improvement plan affecting the top end of his beloved Tilehouse Street had resulted in the demolition the old Free School, a once handsome Jacobean building that had been regarded as a cornerstone of the town's education system. When the new roundabout and road widening had been completed, the local authorities realised they had a small piece of land left over which offered itself as an ideal spot for a memorial garden. It could not have been better placed, being right opposite the birthplace of Hine's Elizabethan hero, the poet and translator George Chapman, and only a stone's throw from the town library and museum that Hine had inspired.

A memorial appeal was launched and quickly produced sufficient money to fund the design and construction of the walled garden that now stands on the old Free School site. Set in the main wall is a plaque that features a bronze relief of Hine's distinctive profile. Beneath his name and credentials is the inscription:

Semper In Libris
Præbuit Speculum Mundi
Always in his books he held up a mirror to the world

One Wednesday afternoon in September 1952, Florence, Felicity and other members of the family joined 150 guests for a service of commemoration led by the town's new vicar, the Reverend Outram Walsh. The plaque was unveiled by the Lord Lieutenant of Hertfordshire, David Bowes Lyon, who told the assembly: 'Reginald Hine might well have become a famous national scholar but instead he chose to devote his life to the service of Hitchin and the county of Hertford ... He was a great and much-loved citizen of this town and here, in this charming little garden, future generations will be able to think of him with an evergreen appreciation.'

Following that ceremony Florence Hine never again set foot

in Hitchin. She had already moved away to West Sussex and, in that same month of September 1952, Willian Bury was sold for £7,000. Although she never felt able to return to the town that held such tragic memories, she enjoyed entertaining old Hertfordshire friends at Brookdene, her new six-bedroom home tucked under the South Downs in the village of Graffham. Among the visitors was her husband's old partner Reginald Hartley, who had given unstinting support during the months following the tragedy. He continued to look after Florence's affairs until his retirement in 1963. Then, with his wife Alice, he moved to Jersey but by that time was already seriously ill with lung cancer. Only a few months later he died in a nursing home in St. Helier at the age of sixty-eight.

One of the curses of manic depression is that it is sometimes passed down through families genetically. It was probably because of this that, in 1958, Florence had to cope with the ordeal of a second suicide in her family; one that bore painful similarities to the death of her husband. Geoffrey Pyman, her brother, had been living with her at Willian Bury since his wife left him in the 1930s. When the house was sold he decided to remain in the area and took a flat at Sollershott Hall in Letchworth. Although he never fully recovered from the emotional shock of being abandoned by his wife and son, he continued to take an active role in the family ship-broking business and enjoyed playing golf and tennis until well into his seventies. As he was approaching his seventy-fifth birthday he was struck down by pneumonia. The illness left him weak and emotionally vulnerable. Then, like his father Frank many years before, he began to suffer bouts of acute depression and was twice admitted to a mental hospital. Each time he discharged himself against medical advice.

Early one Tuesday morning in September 1958, Geoffrey cycled from Letchworth to the village of Great Wymondley, where he stopped at a bridge that crosses the main railway line about a mile-and-a-half south of Hitchin station. After placing his bicycle behind some bushes, he climbed down the embankment and hid behind one of the bridge pillars until he heard a northbound express approaching. The horrified driver saw Geoffrey step out from behind the pillar, look briefly upwards and then dive onto the track in front of the train. No suicide note was found but, at the inquest later, the owner of Sollershott Hall, George Jameson, reported that Geoffrey had recently been worried that he was losing his eyesight. He had also developed 'a great horror' that (like his father) he would have to spend the remainder of his life in an asylum. The jury returned a verdict that he committed suicide while the balance of his mind was disturbed.

Florence died shortly after celebrating her ninety-second birthday. Her great longevity meant that she also outlived her daughter and son-in-law. Felicity and Bill McEwen had returned to England in 1956 when Sudan was granted independence. Bill had a succession of jobs and was for some time general manager of Fison Airwork, running a fleet of crop-spraying helicopters from a base in Cambridgeshire. However, in what would now be considered middle age, both he and Felicity began to suffer poor health as a result of malarial infections contracted during their time in Africa. Both died whilst still in their fifties. Felicity, who had suffered from asthma most of her life, survived her husband by five years, dying in 1973. Despite having to endure such a long string of family tragedies the redoubtable Florence remained bright and positive to the end of her life. She drew great comfort from her three grandsons to whom she had been almost a second mother while their parents were abroad. Andrew, Michael and William, who by then had families of their own, continued to see their grandmother regularly, until her death at Midhurst in December 1980.

The McEwen brothers' work took them to widely differing parts of the world. Following a career in journalism that included a period as Diplomatic Editor of *The Times*, Andrew settled in Italy, where he and his wife Rita opened an English Language school. Michael went to Hong Kong to manage a banknote-printing factory, later retiring to live in New Zealand. William, the youngest, became a farmer in the Orkney Islands. Before leaving England, they paid one more visit to Hertfordshire. On a sunny autumn weekend in 1983 the three families drove up from their homes in London and the Home Counties to rendezvous at the ruins of Minsden chapel [*Illus*.62]. They spent the day clearing the thicket of bushes and scrub that had grown over their grandfather's grave. Aware that vandals had smashed the gravestone some years earlier they took with them a trailer-load of equipment and materials that included gallons of water, some sand and cement. Andrew later wrote:

'The vandals had managed to break the memorial stone into two pieces in such a way that the word *Hitchin* in *Historian of Hitchin* was obliterated. After much scrubbing to remove three decades of grime we laid a deep foundation of concrete and embedded the two pieces in it, marrying them together as best we could. Then we cemented hundreds of flint stones that had fallen from the central arch and walls back into their beds. As a final touch, four of our grandfather's great-grandchildren helped to plant daffodil bulbs in the ruined chancel. When we were clearing up to leave, a gentleman from the local historical society arrived and kindly commended our efforts. We knew that neither he nor we could prevent the ruins from being reclaimed by the thicket in the future, but at least we had transformed a foolish insult into an opportunity to honour our grandfather's memory.'

Twenty-five years on, into the 21st century, the stone is once more covered in grime and barely legible, but at least it is still firmly embedded in its cement base [*Illus*. 61]. Contrary to the family's fears, someone *does* come along from time to time, armed with a pair of shears, to ensure that the grave is not obliterated for all time. Surprisingly, Hine's memorial garden is now quieter and more secluded than when it was first opened. Since the building of a relief road, Tilehouse Street is no longer a thoroughfare and the houses and the garden at the top end are well protected by a high wall and ornamental trees.

For a long time after his death Hine's books had a strangely negative effect on students of history in the town. Such was his renown that, for thirty years, nobody dreamed of writing anything about old Hitchin without quoting him. Publishing a book that dared to offer a fresh look at the town's history would have been considered almost impertinent. Not until the mid-1970s, notably with the founding of Hitchin Historical Society, did local historians reawaken and begin to seek out the wealth of untouched material that still awaited discovery. Since then literally dozens of local books – hardbacks, paperbacks and slim volumes – have been published, bringing to light new and interesting stories about the town and its people.

Although no author has yet matched (or, probably, *wanted* to match) the grandiloquent style and presentation of Hine's books, each has provided one more 'small mirror' through which future generations can take a peep back into the past. Some – myself included – have been surprised to find that, despite Hine's claims of carefully wading through 'hundreds of thousands of charters' and 'thousands of pages of Quaker manuscripts' there are a good number of factual errors in his books. The views of those Edwardian pioneers of the East Herts Archaeological Society, who criticised Hine's early dissertations, have been firmly endorsed by a number of present-day historians. These include two past curators of Hitchin Museum who had no doubt that Hine, as one delicately put it, 'frequently stretched the bounds of probability in the interests of telling a good story.'

Were he still with us, the man in their sights would have delighted in arguing this point with them. He would also have read every new book about the history of his town and gone out of his way to meet and encourage the authors. One writer who publicly lamented Hine's loss in 1949 was a London historian and lecturer named William Kent:

> It was my pleasure to meet Mr Hine from time to time at the British Museum. Twice he entertained me to tea. The memories of those delightful talks at a restaurant in Great Russell Street will be as happy in recollection as was Izaak Walton's chance encounter with Bishop Sanderson amongst the book shops of Little Britain or Charles Lamb's sojourning with Coleridge over potations at the *Salutation and Cat* in Newgate Street. These were real pleasures because Hine seemed to be as interested in his friends' books as in his own, a not too common trait amongst literary men. Almost

all the letters I received contained a gracious compliment for my work . . . In his presence one experienced a sense of real friendship, further conveyed by the clasp of his hand. His old world courtesy and charming personality were endearing qualities, rare in our austere age.

With its timely passing reference to Charles Lamb, Kent's tribute is perhaps the one on which to let this biography finish. After Hine's rather sad account of his night drive across Hertfordshire in a futile attempt to glimpse the ghost of the long-departed *Elia*, it would be satisfying to know that these two have at last met up. The definitive 'Odd Couple,' tramping the highways and byways of their county together. The long-legged Hine striding impatiently ahead as they make their way up the track from Chapelfoot to the tranquil ruins of Minsden. The tiny Lamb having to break into a trot from time to time to keep up with his loquacious companion:

> 'Lamb, my dear fellow, you *must* come and see where they scattered me. Did you know that I once owned this heavenly haunt and actually completed writing my *Confessions* upon this hill? I had hoped to die here you know. 'Passing deliciously from peace to peace,' was how I put it – rather neatly, I would submit. Unfortunately events did not turn out in quite the way I had planned ... Now ... just look at that sublime view of our native fields of Hertfordshire!'

THE LOST BELLS OF MINSDEN

Epilogue from a Grandson
'Viewed in a faded mirror'

Andrew McEwen was six years old when his grandfather died. As the oldest of the three grandsons, he is the last member of the family who is able to recollect snatches of life at Willian Bury during the final year of Reginald Hine's life. Although some of these memories are fleeting and indistinct they have a mystical touch about them, suggesting that the historian's fascination with paranormal events may not have ended with his death.

* * *

WHAT AWOKE ME in the dead of night I cannot recall, or perhaps never knew. A footstep? A shadow? Perhaps the creak of a floorboard? All that now seems certain is that my awakening was sudden, and with it came an awareness of not being alone. This was not unusual, for I was blessed with parents and grandparents who cared enough to look into my room at night. For a while I lay awake listening to the silence of the big house, without opening my eyes to see who was with me. Not a murmur came from my parents' cluttered bedroom to my right; nothing stirred in my grandmother's room on the other side.

No doubt my thoughts were absorbed by the whispered command I had overheard before bedtime: 'Don't tell the children.' No doubt I was struggling to make sense of the sudden commotion at Willian Bury, our lovely rambling home, earlier that day; of the meaningful glances that my parents had not wanted me to notice. I say 'no doubt' because fifty-eight years have passed since the incident I am about to recall and, while my memory of the central element is clear, some details are hazy, including precisely when it happened.

Although not yet seven years old, I was not too young to piece together the evidence. A stranger at the door, furtive conversations between my parents, my grandmother and Stella our nanny, the shock and distress on the grown-ups' faces. That evening our parents, but not my grandmother, were present while we three boys had supper. I remember the look on my parents' faces when we asked where Grandpa was and the vague answer about his having 'gone to Jesus,' or something similar. Yes, the fact of Reginald Hine's death must have been clear to his eldest grandchild, even if the adults had successfully concealed the terrible details. How else to explain my terror when I opened my eyes and found him sitting in the armchair opposite my bed, looking at me intently, illuminated by the soft amber nightlight in my room? Why should I have been frightened if I thought he were alive?

I pulled the eiderdown over my head, slunk down beneath the bedclothes, braced my feet against the stout wooden bedposts, and remained there for hours, not daring to peep out. Even now, more than half a century later, the fear I experienced that night remains vivid. Fear and confusion, for the man I had seen, although unmistakably my grandfather, was somehow changed, as if viewed in a faded mirror. This was no longer the kindly Grandpa I loved and who loved me, the Grandpa who would occasionally let me sit in his study watching him as he worked; what I saw was a distorted reflection of Reginald Hine.

The following morning I felt unable to tell anyone what had happened; I was old enough to realise that such a report would earn me a scolding from my parents. My brother Michael, two years younger, was perhaps not yet aware that safety lay in silence. Years later my mother would recall that he had reported seeing my grandfather after his death, and had been firmly reprimanded for speaking nonsense. Michael now has only a second-hand memory of this, based on what our mother said rather than his own recollections, but it does seem that we had somewhat similar experiences. He also recalls (though this may have been a separate incident) that he awoke one night and found that he was in the presence of a benign being. At the time he assumed that this was an angel, and did not feel afraid.

Dreams, you will say, indeed dreams with simple psychological implications. Do I protest? No, I accept that you are probably right, though at the time the experience was so extraordinary and compelling that I should entirely have excluded the possibility of it being a dream. But if I now accept that I may have been wrong, that what occurred may have been nothing more than the ramblings of a child's sleep-intoxicated mind, why give it prominence? The reason is that nothing fascinated Reginald Hine more than the borderlands between half-consciousness and the paranormal.

Whatever happened that night – be it a vivid dream or a posthumous visitation by my grandfather – I do not mean to suggest that Willian Bury was haunted. Our home was not without its shadowy corners; its mysterious corridors, its rattling windows and doors that banged eerily when the wind stirred the tall trees in the spinney behind the house. To be sure the lofty windows in the drawing room had a forbidding aspect from the perspective of a small boy. The junk room crammed with abandoned curiosities held unlimited potential for childish fantasy and the secret passage in the cellar, whose destination was then an unexplored subterranean enigma, must have seemed a physical link with the unknown. Equally rich in potential for the infantile imagination was the clump of dark trees near the front door of the house, overhanging the circular drive where my grandparents turned their cars, not to mention the corrugated-iron air raid shelter at the edge of the spinney, with its dank atmosphere and damp floor. Yes, the ingredients were there – the ingredients, but not the pie. Willian Bury was anything but spooky to the mind of a small boy.

Although I later learned that he was plagued by depression, my memories of my grandfather are of a cheerful, warm, kindly person. A tolerant one too, in that he would let me sit with him in his study and complicate his clutter, deploying my tin soldiers upon the battlefield of his desk, among quills, inkpots, magnifying glasses, seals and mountains of documents, watching while he wrote. The opening remark of his *Confessions*, in which he vowed to 'tidy up the overcrowded curiosity shop of my mind,' was a humorous nod to those in the family who demanded a little more order in his study. I did not then know that I was much honoured; my grandfather preferred to be alone when writing and my presence can hardly have been conducive to his prose.

Concealed from me were his terrible private moments, the acid sensation in the mouth and throat, the feeling of an immense weight pressing about the head, the medicines for depression. The side of him that I saw was the light-hearted one: the grandfather who would cheerily greet each member of the family before the rest of us were half out of our slumbers and would then proceed to salute the tapestry of St Vincent that hung in the hall. Such was the family silence about his death that I was in my teens before I knew that he had thrown himself under a train at Hitchin Station.

Whether he does indeed rest in peace I cannot tell you, for he has not taken the trouble to tell me. For a man who believed in the power of the dead to communicate with the living, this is most remiss. Perhaps I complain too much, however, for he did at least offer me the benefit of his professional wisdom. Or, to be more precise, a medium gave me a message with a legal content, purportedly from him. I shall report the facts and you may tell me that I am a fool to commit such tittle-tattle to print.

My wife Rita and I were persuaded by a friend to attend a Spiritualist church service at the village of Chawton, near Alton in Hampshire. I was reluctant, having no belief in spiritualism, but at the same time did not wish to offend our friend. At first the proceedings followed the pattern of a normal Anglican service, but then a middle-aged lady stood up and began delivering messages to members of the congregation, apparently from their departed loved ones. I was not then aware that she was a well-known medium, but had I heard of her I doubt that my initial impression would have been any less unfavourable. Sitting in a pew half hidden from the medium by a pillar, I watched the proceedings with dismay, feeling that conjuring tricks with the departed had no place in a Christian church.

'There is a man behind that pillar who thinks all this is nonsense,' she said. Then she addressed me directly: 'I have a message for you. Your grandfather is standing next to me.' She proceeded to give an accurate physical description of Reginald Hine, who seemed to be dressed in very formal and very old-fashioned attire. Up to that point my scepticism was undiminished. She then said: 'He is a lawyer, and he has a message for you.' This was more surprising, as I had never heard of her before, and so far as I know she had never heard of me. The message was what one might expect a lawyer to say, some advice to be very careful if I had to enter into a contract in the future. There was nothing so specific and personal that it could only have come from Reginald Hine, although I did in fact go through a difficult period in my life many years later as a result of paying insufficient heed to this advice.

It was hard to know what to make of this event, but given that no money changed hands, given that there was no apparent ulterior motive for her intervention, given that the two specific pieces of information she gave (Hine's occupation and his physical stature) were accurate and that the rest was plausible, and given that my grandfather believed in communication with the dead, I felt I should not dismiss the matter out of hand. I could not confidently assert that this was nonsense.

Reginald Hine will be remembered for as long as the living keep turning his pages, but if we would understand him better we should ask what fuelled the curiosity that prompted his literary output. That driving force, I suggest, was the unusual nature of his spirituality. Here was a man who would cheerfully keep company with priests, who rented a ruined chapel as a place to meditate, who once spent a whole night in a church, who devoted huge amounts of time to the study of various Christian denominations, but who refused to commit himself to any of them. Here was a man who felt a powerful bond with something beyond this life, and yet found religion an unsatisfactory means of expressing his spirituality.

Had he lived in the computer era I think Reginald Hine might have described religions as programmes of the spirit, offering convenient ways of channelling a fundamental aspect of human nature, but not necessarily illuminating the nature of the eternal unknown. The motor of his soul was thus a yearning to make better sense of the spirituality that he felt, to look beyond the spiritual programmes that he found so unsatisfactory and incomplete, while his fascination with the paranormal sprang from a wish to probe the nearer shores of the hereafter. Ultimately he longed to know, as perhaps we all do, whether anything lay beyond the void on the far side of that platform at Hitchin Station.

ANDREW MCEWEN
Stagno Lombardo, Cremona, Italy

BIBLIOGRAPHY

The Books and Essays of Reginald Hine

The Manor of Newnham (1910)
Anima Celtica (1912)
Dreams and The Way of Dreams (1913)
The History of Hitchin Volume 1 (1927)
Samuel Lucas, His Life and Art-Work (1928)
The History of Hitchin Volume 2 (1929)
A Mirror for the Society of Friends The Story of the Hitchin
    Quakers (1929)
A Short History of St. Mary's Church, Hitchin (1930)
History of Hitchin Grammar School (1931)
Hitchin Worthies (1932)
The Natural History of the Hitchin Region (1934)
The Story of Methodism in Hitchin (1934)
The Story of the Sun Hotel (1937)
The Story of Hitchin Town, drawings by Gerard Ceunis (1938)
Confessions of an Un-Common Attorney (1945)
Hitchin Old and New Photographs & Drawings (1946)
Hitchin Countryside Photographs & Drawings (1947)
Charles Lamb & His Hertfordshire (1949)
Relics of An Un-common Attorney (1951)

Select List of Sources

Ashby, M., *Stevenage History & Guide* (2002)
Beresford R., *John Beresford's Journal (1931-32)* Parson
    Woodforde Society
Bloom, U., *Parson Extraordinary* (1963)

Brunt, A.W. *Pageant of Letchworth 1903-1914* (1942)

Foster, A. M., *The Book of Hitchin* (1981)

Harvey, W.F., *The Beast with Five Fingers and other Midnight Tales*, (1945)

Hitchcock, S.T., *Mad Mary Lamb: Lunacy and Murder in Literary London* (2005)

Hogg, P & Appleyard, H., *The Pyman Story, Fleet and Family History*

Hordern Sir M., & England P., *A World Elsewhere*, (1993)

Latchmore, E.A., *People, Places and Past Times of Hitchin* (1974)

Letters from Reginald Hine to James Curry (1929-49) Hertford County Archive

Miller, Dr M., *Letchworth - The First Garden* City (1989)

Moore E.T., Poole, H. & Fleck, A., *Old Hitchin* (1976)

Pettigrew, J., Reynolds, R. & Rouse. S., *A Place in the Country: Three Counties Asylum 1860-1998.* (1998)

Pigram, R., *Old Hitchin Life*, Hitchin Historical Society (1983)

Robson M., *Hitchin Quakers Ancient & Modern* A published lecture (2002)

Sheldrick, A. *A Different World – Ashwell before 1939* (1991)

Unwin, P., *The Publishing Unwins*, (1972)

ACKNOWLEDGEMENTS

As well as all those contributors, named and anonymous, who have recorded their memories of Reginald Hine, the author is particularly indebted to the following individuals and organisations for their valuable help and encouragement while he was researching and writing this biography:

Iain Bain, for many years responsible for publishing at the Tate Gallery, London, who designed and produced this book; Dr Michael Clarke, consultant psychiatrist; Mrs Stella Edwards; Mrs Sarah Graham; David Heymans, senior partner of Hawkins Russell Jones, solicitors; Andrew McEwen, oldest grandson of Reginald Hine; William Tudor John, High Sheriff of Hertfordshire, and Mrs Tudor John of Willian Bury;

Also: Robert F. Ashby; Martin Brayne, Chairman of the Parson Woodforde Society; Joan Catteau; Nick Connell, assistant at the Archives and Local Studies Centre, County Hall, Hertford; Neil Cornwell; First Garden City Heritage Museum, Letchworth, and their documentation officer Josh Tidy; Alan Fleck; Hitchin Girls' School Archive and Priscilla Douglas; David Hodges, curator, and his colleagues at Hitchin Museum; Christina Mackwell of Lambeth Palace Library; Eric T. Moore; the Old Leysian Union, Cambridge and their secretary John Harding; Stuart Sanders; and Karen White, B.B.C. Written Archives Centre.

ILLUSTRATIONS

The author would also like to thank Simon Coxall who edited and enhanced many of the illustrations for this book. Also the following for allowing the reproduction of photographs and illustrations in their possession:

Margaret Ashby (44); First Garden City Heritage Museum (Frontispiece, 43, 53, 54); Sarah Graham (56); Hawkins Russell Jones (23); Hine family archives (5, 10-14, 16, 17, 20, 22, 25-28, 30, 35-39, 40, 42, 45, 46, 55, 57, 59, 62); Hitchin Museum (4, 19, 21, 29, 33, 47, 48, 60, 64-66); Terry Knight (2 & 3); Stuart Sanders (49); Dr Gerry Tidy (24 & 34). The remaining photographs are from the author's own collection.

The composite photograph on the front of the dust jacket was created by Michael Inns, of Mixed Images, Hitchin. Hine's silhouette on page 210 was drawn in 1952 by Mr Harold Pettingale, Deputy Surveyor of Hitchin Urban District Council, who designed the bronze relief for the plaque in the Hine Memorial Garden.

LIST OF SUBSCRIBERS

Mr & Mrs Martin Alcock
Jonathan Andrews
Mrs Joan Armstrong
Margaret Ashby
Robert F. & Jeane M. Ashby
John Austin

Robert & Lesley Bacon
Jonathan Barnes
Alan Beaumont
Mavis & David Bell
Mrs J. M. Bennett
Trevor Bentham
Jacky Birch
Tony & Rae Bliss
Adrian M. Bowyer
Walter James Boxer
Stephen Bradford-Best
Martin Brayne
Paul & Rosemary Brenham
D. Bridges
H. M. Brigham
Janet Brooker
Martin Brunt
Hugh Buckle
Claire Bunyan & Andy Rodgers
Paul, Diana & Madeleine Burns
Maurice Burr
Gordon Burton
Kenneth K. Burton

Peter & Catherine Camfield
Andrew Carmichael
Mr A.B. & Mrs I.J. Castledine

Joan Catteau
Jane & Jeremy Cave
David & Catherine Chamberlain
Mrs D.M. Chamberlain
David & Juliette Chamberlain
Michael Chamberlin
Ann Chambers
Alan & Sue Chandler
Leslie Chandler
Mrs Rita Chapple
Peter & Joan Cherry
Mr & Mrs G.F. Clark
John W. Clark
Mike & Ellie Clarke
Jean Coad
Nicholas Connell
David & Susan Cook
Jackie Cooper
Neil Cornwell
Celia & Mike Cowling
Sidney W.R. Cox o.b.e.
John & Margaret Coxall
Alan Cudmore
Mr R. & Mrs P. Cutler

Gordon Day
Philip & Betty Day
Priscilla Douglas
Stephen Dyer

Stella Edwards
A.R.G. Else
D.G. Else
J.C.E. Else

Leslie & Lucy Farley
J.D. Farnworth
Ron & Hilda Farr
A. Fisher & Family
Joyce & John Fisher
Kirk R.S. Foster
Julie Foulds & Nail Turk
Hannah French (née McEwen)
    and Marcus, Isabel & Thomas
    McEwen
Brian & Dilys Freeman
Charlie Frost (*In Memoriam*)
Graham Frost

John Gardiner
Michael Gilbertson
Mark & Helen Gimson
Keith & Juliet Glazebrook
Gregory & Angela Gould
Sir Alexander Graham G.B.E.
Mrs Janet Grant

Andrew Haigh
Sanda & Adrian Haigh
Pamela Gladys Hailey (*In
    Memoriam*)
Fiona Jane Haines
Master Cooper Haines
Stuart Halsey
Mr Dennis A. Hammond
Ray & Angela Hammond
Anne Hampson
Lillian Hare
Betty Harkness
Peter & Margaret Harkness
Philip & Wendy Harkness
Robert & Edda Harkness

Jean Harris (née Rogers)
Joan D. Hart
Paul & Marion Hartnack
Hawkins Russell Jones
C. & J.A. Healey
David & Ann Heymans
Peter Highton
Elizabeth Hill
Andrew Hine
Mrs Ann Hine
Charles Hine
Edward Burgass Hine
Dr & Mrs J.L. Hine
Air Chief Marshal Sir Patrick
    Hine
Mrs Peter C. Hine
Hitchin Boys' School Library
Hitchin Historical Society
Mr & Mrs T.C. Holme
Mark & Linda Holt
Nigel Holt
John & Anne Hope
Keith Hoskins
David & Bridget Howlett
Mr & Mrs L.E. Hughes
Pauline Humphries
Mr James W. Hunter
Pat & Norman Hyde

Ian & Georghia
Anthony Charles Allen Ireland
Sir Stephen Irwin
John Izzard

John & Doreen Jarvis
Derek & Audrey Jenkins
Mr & Mrs G. Jenkins

Douglas & Maureen Kell
Brenda M. King
Julian Kowalik

Anthony J. Lambert
G. Lambert
P.J. Lawlor
George & Peggy Lawrence
Phil & Ita Leaver
John Leeson
Robin & Janice Lilly
Mrs James Lindsell
Mrs M. Lisser
Mrs Margaret Lomas
Julian W. Lovelace
Stella Lupson

Stuart MacDonald
Stephen MacSweeney
Ann & John Males
Mr C.C. Males
Bernard & Beryl Mallett
Christopher M. Mann
M.J. & M. Matthews
Anthony Maxim
Diane Maybank & Bill Sellicks
Geoff Mayes
May & Ian McArthur
Andrew, Rita & Amelia McEwen
Johnny, Megan, Aida & Violet
    McEwen
Kelsall, Thea, William & Flora
    McEwen
Luke, Sylvia & Toby McEwen
Michael J. L. McEwen
Samuel, Jill & Ivy McEwen
Sebastian, Ruth, Nadia & Toby
    McEwen

William & Sandy McEwen
Mrs Ferguson McNeill
A. W. & J. P. Mead
Chris Mennie & Suzanne Currie
Mrs Pansy Mitchell
David Mole
Geoffrey & Linda Monk
Bernard & Nenna Moore
Eric T. Moore & Margaret
    Moore
Stephen R. Moore
David & Jan Morgan
Sarah & Russell Morris
Margaret S. Morton

Allan & Shirley Newey
Barry Newland
Denise & Alan Newland
Mr & Mrs A. J. Norgan
Hugh Northam

Lady Osborn (Patricia)
Geoff & Alvina Oxley

Ken Page
Michael Page
Mark Andrew Pardoe
Clough Park
Stephen Parker
Andrew & Deirdre Parr
Martin & Patience Pascal
Mr & Mrs J.C. Pearce
Dr M.J. Peel
Anthony & Anitra Perry
Tony Phillips & Martha Ross-
    Phillips
Colin Philpott

David Philpott
Roy & Daphne Pike
Adrian & Hazel Pomfret
John & Jean Pomfret
Frank & Edith Pratt
Paul & Gill Pritchard
Judd & Jean Procter
Fiona Pyman

Anne & Jim Raill
Tim Ray
Karen & Tony Ridout
Peter & Barbara Robbins
Peter & Helen Roberts
Lucy, Damian, Ziggy & Jago
    Roberts
Eric V. Rogers
David Ross
Phil Rowe & Val Campion
Mr & Mrs H. Russell

Mr Brendan Salisbury
Stuart & Eileen Sanders
Jane, Chris, Jack & Beth
    Saunders
John S. Scorer
Raymond Scroggins
Eric Sharp
Gillian Shaw
John & Judy Simmonds
Brian & Pamela Simpkins
Leslie & Jean Simpkins
Pam & Ray Skeggs
Miss C. M. Spicer

Kate, Klaus, Charlie & Harvey
    Steed
John M. Stoddard J.P.
Janet & John Stonehouse

G. W. Thake
Steve, Amy & Freddie Thomas
Mike & Lesley Thurman
Dr Gerry Tidy
Bill & Jane Tudor John

Revd W.S. & Mrs W. Upchurch

Albert Vaughan (*In Memoriam*)
Dr & Mrs John Vick

Simon & Janet Walker
John & Janet Walton
Howard F. Webber
Jane White
E.P. Whitehead
Anne Williams
Hugh Williams
Jean & John Williams
Joyce & Frank Williams
Robin Williams
Jennifer & Lewis Willis
David & Jacqui Willock
Maureen & David Wilson
Sarah, Richard & Alfie Withers
Marion & David Woodbridge
Richard C. Worbey
Rodney & Judith Wray

R.F. Zimmern

INDEX